The

UNDISTRACTED

WIDOW

The

UNDISTRACTED WIDOW

LIVING FOR GOD AFTER LOSING YOUR HUSBAND

CAROL W. CORNISH

CROSSWAY

WHEATON, ILLINOIS

Cover design: Faceout Studio, www.faceoutstudio.com

Cover photo: Millennium Images Ltd.

First printing 2010

Printed in the United States of America

Trade paperback ISBN: 978-1-4335-1232-2
PDF ISBN: 978-1-4335-1233-9
Mobipocket ISBN: 978-1-4335-1234-6
ePub ISBN: 978-1-4335-2362-5

Library of Congress Cataloging-in-Publication Data

Cornish, Carol, 1945–
   The undistracted widow : living for God after losing your husband /
Carol Cornish.
     p. cm.
   Includes bibliographical references (p.   ).
   ISBN: 978-1-4335-1232-2 (tpb)
   1. Consolation. 2. Widows—Religious life. 3. Bereavement—Religious aspects—Christianity. I. Title.
BV4908.C66   2010
248.8'434—dc22
                                        2010001693

Crossway is a publishing ministry of Good News Publishers.

VP		20	19	18	17	16	15	14	13	12	11	10
15	14	13	12	11	10	9	8	7	6	5	4	3	2	1

In loving memory of
ROLLY CORNISH
and to
Emma Jane, Suzy Anne, and Andrew Darren,
who, though they will not know their Granddad on this earth,
I pray by God's grace will meet him in heaven.

CONTENTS

ACKNOWLEDGMENTS

My sincere thanks to:

Elisabeth Elliot, whose writings on grief and widowhood gave seed to this book.

Elyse Fitzpatrick, whose persistent encouragement helped to make this book possible.

John Muhlfeld, my pastor, whose steadfast prayers, kind encouragement, and pastoral perspective on the manuscript gave me confidence in going forward.

Diane Tyson and Michelle Wright, who read an earlier version of the manuscript and gave valuable suggestions and insights, and whose love and prayers made a huge difference as I worked.

Karen Aaron, my sister twice over, whose prayers, daily phone calls, and helpful feedback showered me with love.

My son, Darren, whose love and support have always meant so much to me. I see your dad in your eyes.

Family and friends who regularly asked about my work and prayed for me.

Lydia Brownback, whose enthusiasm for the work, sweet encouragement, and skill as an editor made this book so much better.

INTRODUCTION

Marriage is the most intimate of human relationships. When that relationship is severed by death, intense sorrow follows. I was surprised at the uniqueness and depth of this grief. Over a period of five years, I also lost my father, my mother, my aunt, and my father-in-law. None of these losses, however, compared in intensity to the grief of losing my husband.

My husband died in the late fall, and I distinctly remember being surprised when spring came that I was still alive. I never thought I would make it through the winter. I don't mean that I was suicidal, but each day was so hard that I thought I would just wear out. Now, several years later, I can tell you with full assurance from the Scriptures and from my experience that God can bring you to a place of contentment. You can faithfully endure the winter of your grief if you lean on the Lord for all you need. It is my fervent hope and sincere prayer that this book will encourage your hurting heart and uplift your soul.

The loss of one's husband can be disorienting. Christian wives often are accustomed to living every day responding to their husband's leadership and, consequently, his absence creates a huge vacuum. We Christian widows must embrace the comforting reality that Christ was and still is the head of our home. We need to learn moment by moment, day by day, to live not on our own but in response to Christ. Our husband is no longer here to fulfill his leadership responsibility, but the Spirit of Christ will continue to provide leadership in our home.

John Angell James, writing in the nineteenth century, noted the availability to mourners of general works concerning consolation in affliction, but he lamented the lack of any work prepared to particularly comfort widows. This observation was the inspiration for his book entitled *The Widow Directed to the Widow's God*.[1] It is an excellent work but challenging to read due to archaic language and an antiquated writing style.

Many contemporary books address the subject of suffering and grief in general. I found some of them helpful. I found it wearisome, however, to sort through them, trying to make application to my particular suffering after I was widowed. The effort to do so seemed Herculean in the exhaustion of grief.

I've long been accustomed to putting my thoughts on paper. In addition, my counselor training emphasized the writing of plans to work out strategies for overcoming problems. So, it seemed natural when I faced the monumental task of adjusting to life as a widow to write it all down and fashion a plan for myself. My plan grew and grew and my notebook got so full that I couldn't get the large-ring binder to close. Over the last several years, I've turned repeatedly to this material to find comfort, courage, strength, and hope to go on from one day to the next. The book you now hold in your hands grew out of that plan. I long for you to find in the following pages readily available comfort, compassionate understanding, and real hope.

I want to tell you enough of my story to assure you of my empathy with your grief. But then I want to step aside and point you to Christ, for he is able to come alongside you by the presence of his Spirit. He cares for you. He wants you to know him better. Times of deep sorrow can produce in us a profound sense of loneliness, but if we set our eyes of faith on Christ and seek to know him in the midst of pain, he will give us a clearer vision of who he is and who we are in him. The Lord Jesus Christ can give us confidence in him so strong that we can face anything because he is with us.

Someday the torrent of tears will slow to occasional trickles. Someday the pain in your heart will fade. Someday you will look back and see how far God has brought you. May this book help you to find true comfort and real strength to keep walking with the Lord for his glory and your good as you reach toward that day.

1

BEGINNING, ENDING, AND BEGINNING AGAIN

For everything there is a season, and a time for every matter under heaven:
a time to be born, and a time to die;
a time to plant, and a time to pluck up what is planted; . . .
a time to weep, and a time to laugh; a time to mourn,
and a time to dance.

ECCLESIASTES 3:1–2, 4

The discomfort in his right side started late in the summer. Since several family members had wrestled with gallbladder troubles, my husband assumed he was facing surgery at worst, diet changes at best. As his pains persisted, we went to a surgeon who ordered tests but was not alarmed at the symptoms. Follow-up appointments got delayed several times as the surgeon faced serious health problems of his own. Finally, after the third delay, we switched surgeons. This doctor took a more serious and aggressive approach to the problem.

THE BEGINNING OF THE END

Chest X-rays, MRIs, CT scans—the data was collected and the unthinkable climbed to the top of the pile of possibilities. Lung cancer! My husband had never smoked. A tumor the size of a golf ball was present in his right lung. Other smaller tumors were splattered over the lining of the lung like slush on a windshield. Shock is too mild a word for what we felt when we got the news in a phone call. We sat together, held each other, and sobbed.

A biopsy confirmed the diagnosis as adenocarcinoma. My husband underwent surgery in mid-January, and a difficult postoperative period began. Though we were told his pain would last six to eight weeks, he was in pain for the rest of his life—eleven months. The oncologist held out hope that he might have two years left to live or perhaps even longer. The day my husband died, two hospice workers visited him in our home, one in the morning and one in the early evening. That same day he was able to walk a short distance, talk to people visiting, and endure various treatments. But around 6:00 p.m., I noticed some troubling changes. I took the hospice nurse aside and pointedly asked her if he was dying. She responded that he was not actively dying, but five hours later he was dead.

Medical workers can try to estimate the time of death but only God knows when we will die. Approximately three hours after the hospice nurse left, my husband's pain increased dramatically. I frantically called the hospice and pleaded with them to send another nurse, but they did not consent to my request. I hung up and immediately called for an ambulance, but within minutes my husband took his last breaths. It was unreal. I am grateful to God that my husband died at home, as he wished, and not in the hospital. I saw God powerfully at work that night.

I was blessed that most of my extended family lives nearby. Having two of my sisters-in-law present when my husband died was comforting. They are sweet, thoughtful women, and it was good not to be alone. I called our son to tell him his dad had died. How utterly devastating it was to lose his father! There is something profoundly sad about hearing a strong young man cry—such a juxtaposition of physical strength and emotional fragility, a desire to be strong and a shattered heart. We were up all night.

Family members and friends provided every needed comfort during and after my husband's illness and death. One friend stayed with me for several nights immediately after my husband's death. What a comfort to be with a mature Christian woman who knew when to speak and when to be silent! She gently pointed me to the Lord for comfort, prayed with me, and reminded me of the hope we have in Christ both for this life and the life to come. In my exhaustion, it was a significant help to have someone reminding me of these things.

At the funeral service, my pastor blessed us with a message that comforted the afflicted and afflicted the comfortable. I was thankful for his words. He didn't waste the opportunity to tell the truth of the gospel.[1] Then we drove to the cemetery for the graveside service. It was a sunny day but sharply cold. I stepped out of the limousine and took my son's arm. As we approached the grave, the funeral director motioned for us to sit in that place where none of us want to find ourselves—the front row—the next of kin. I could barely contain my sobs and silently prayed for strength. This was it. The body consigned to the ground. No more lingering hugs, no warm holding of hands, no sweet kisses from lips that I knew so well, no more sparkle in hazel eyes that twinkled with mischievous humor. I praise God that I will see my husband again some day. I don't know how long that will be, but God knows, and that makes it all right.

EVENINGS AND WEEKENDS

Though my husband passed on, my life continued. During daylight hours I was okay, but as the sun set and the winter darkness fell around me, it seemed as if the walls moved closer together. At that time of day I was incredulous that my husband was gone. When I started to cry, I wondered how I would ever stop.

> Be gracious to me, O LORD, for I am in distress;
> > my eye is wasted from grief;
> > my soul and my body also.
> For my life is spent with sorrow,
> > and my years with sighing. (Ps. 31:9–10)

It helped to read aloud verses of Scripture and texts of hymns (I scarcely had enough breath to speak, much less sing). These verses from a hymn helped soothe my aching soul:

> Does Jesus care when my way is dark with a nameless dread and fear?
> As the daylight fades into deep night shades, does He care enough
> > to be near?
> Does Jesus care when I've said "goodbye" to the dearest on earth to me,
> > and my sad heart aches till it nearly breaks, Is it aught to Him?
> > Does He see?

Oh yes, He cares, I know He cares, his heart is touched with my grief;
when the days are weary the long nights dreary, I know my Savior cares.[2]

Jesus cares and he comforts. Recently, I realized that I no longer have large boxes of tissues in every room. Progress, definite progress.

Weekends were difficult to get through and still can be at times, though I do see progress there also. I need to accept a whole different rhythm to my life and to gladly accept it week by week. A friend who is a missionary in Europe and is single counseled me to start my own new traditions. By this she meant that I needed to form new patterns to my days and weeks and months and years. I understood I would need to do this in regard to holidays, but my friend showed me I needed new routines even for ordinary days.

CHECKING OFF A DIFFERENT BOX

I was my husband's caretaker for the year he lived after his diagnosis. I watched as more downs than ups finally claimed his life. The world couldn't be without him in it, could it? We met in high school, dated through college, and married soon after graduation. I've often thought about the biblical teaching regarding the spouse of your youth. It's special, that young love, and more so as the years go by and love matures. Friends for forty-five years—friends like that don't go away, do they? Lovers for thirty-eight years—can love like that leave my life?

Yes, it can. It did. Now I'm single again. Now I'm something I never expected to be. (I should have been more realistic.) I'm a widow. The first time I checked off "widow" on a form it conjured up images of frail old ladies dressed in black, sitting in rocking chairs, and staring blankly into nowhere. It led me to recall a Dylan Thomas story. Referring to elderly aunts he writes, "And some few small aunts, not wanted in the kitchen, nor anywhere else for that matter, sat on the very edges of their chairs, poised and brittle, afraid to break, like faded cups and saucers."[3] I felt like I could break. Would I?

Periods of intense grief become fewer and farther between as we learn to put our trust in God and walk by faith, not by sight. It's like driving in patchy fog early in the morning. The murkiness clears and you cover some distance, then meet with reduced visibility again until the sun burns off the fog and the road is clear ahead. It's vital not to lose sight of the Lord as we travel this misty path. God is watching over us with eyes of empathy and love. "When we lift our inward eyes to gaze upon God, we are sure to meet friendly eyes gazing back at us. When the eyes of the soul looking out meet the eyes of God looking in, heaven has begun right here on this earth."[4] We need grace to set our mind's eye on the Lord and not to take it off. He knows our suffering and longs to comfort us in it. He is not distant or uncaring. He doesn't want us to travel the foggy road alone. He can and will help us in every way.

GOD'S INVOLVEMENT

Widowhood is not simply a problem to be solved or a circumstance that must somehow be overcome. Because God is sovereign over all things, he is in control of our situation for his glory and our good. I found a helpful article by Geoff Thomas while searching for materials with which to counsel myself. It is entitled "Singleness." If you are newly widowed, this article may be hard to read but nonetheless encouraging. Thomas gives us a godly perspective by explaining that singleness is a calling from God:

> Both marriage and singleness are callings, or vocations. The idea of *calling*, or *vocation*, is not one we often use, but it is very significant. When we view our lives as a calling from God, we believe that God has arranged for us to enter a certain state, and God qualifies us to live in that state, and God will use us in that state to bring in the kingdom of God. That is also true for the Christian whose spouse has died, and it is true for the Christian whose spouse has walked out and deserted him or her. Now you have a vocation from God to be single. That is your calling and you can live positively and productively as a single person; you were once single and glorified God by that, and then you were married and you glorified God by that and now you are single again, and that was not bad luck or chance but the will of God, a good gift from the Lord. Jesus said that anyone who can accept this gift should accept it. Let me say quickly that to be sure, no one would expect such a person to think about the advantages of singleness immediately after some traumatic event that has made him or her single, but God reigns and God keeps us all.[5]

You see, the primary reason we are here is to bring glory to God. We are workers in his kingdom. This life is not principally about comfort or enjoyment as we define them but as God defines them for us.

For over twenty years, I've been ministering to women and their families as a biblical counselor. I've also been teaching women's Bible studies. My seminary education and church ministry experience were lifesavers during my husband's illness and after his death. During this time I started journaling. I emphasized in my writing those things for which I could thank God each day. By doing this I was better able to keep my eyes on Christ and on the good things God was doing during these trials. I commend the practice of journaling to you.

I hope in this book you will find blessing in the things the Lord used to comfort and encourage me. God has no favorites. What he did for me he can do for you. May your heart be strengthened and your soul soothed by God's Word and Spirit. The Lord specializes in providing comfort to those who find themselves at breaking points. I am eager to tell you how he kept me from breaking and even brought me to the point of incandescent joy in him in the midst of bereavement.

> Be still, my soul: the Lord is on your side;
> bear patiently the cross of grief or pain;
> leave to your God to order and provide;
> in ev-'ry change he faithful will remain.
> Be still, my soul: your best, your heav'n-ly Friend
> through thorny ways leads to a joyful end.[6]

2

IDENTIFYING YOURSELF ANEW

But by the grace of God I am what I am, and his grace toward me was not in vain. On the contrary, I worked harder than any of them, though it was not I, but the grace of God that is with me.

1 CORINTHIANS 15:10

In the past, the word *widow* conjured up all kinds of negative images in my mind—black clothing, sad looks, desperate sighs, and whispered comments.

A ROSE BY ANY OTHER NAME

My first experience knowing a widow was as a small child. I remember thinking there was something different about my great-aunt. (All my other aunts were connected to an uncle.) My great-uncle had died, and I heard her called a "widow." Whatever that meant, I could sense it wasn't a good thing. It was kept quiet, whispered.

By dictionary definition, a widow is a woman who has lost her husband by death and has not married again. According to the U.S. Census Bureau, in 2006 there were over eleven million widows in this country.[1] I was astonished when I first saw that number. After joining the ranks of those millions, I searched for some books that would comfort and instruct me. But, with the exception of a small booklet by Elisabeth Elliot and a book written in 1841, I couldn't find anything that specifically and significantly spoke to my experience. As a result, I began counseling myself by writing down things that resonated with what I was going through and offered the comfort of God's Word. I wanted to know what God's Word said about widows. I needed to inform my mind and organize scriptural

21

teaching about widowhood so I could understand and learn from it. All of us interpret what is happening to us, and I wanted my interpretations to flow from God's truth.

It's essential to look first into God's Word. If we begin elsewhere, we will not know how to think biblically about widowhood. By "thinking biblically," I mean that we must know what God says so we can think his thoughts after him. This is the path to blessing and real help. I was desperate to find out how God would meet me in my sorrow and loneliness. God says much in his Word about the condition and care of widows. We will consider some verses now and others in subsequent chapters.

YOUR IDENTITY IN CHRIST

According to the Scriptures, our identity as Christians flows *primarily* from the fact that we are children of God, adopted into his family and saved from an eternity in hell because his Son, Jesus, died in our place to pay the penalty for our sin. God is our heavenly Father, and we belong to him and to our Savior: "Father, I desire that they also, whom you have given me, may be with me where I am, to see my glory that you have given me because you loved me before the foundation of the world" (John 17:24). The Scriptures direct us to think of ourselves in this way. God's Word uses other metaphors to describe those who belong to God, but "child" or "son" is the principal description and the most endearing.[2] You may have a more difficult time adjusting to life without your spouse if in the past you primarily thought of yourself as a wife. Please don't misunderstand—being a wife is a wonderful gift from God and a significant privilege. But if your understanding of yourself was largely attached to that role, then when you lose that role you lose a strong sense of who you are.

Several months after my husband died, I was sitting with a friend sipping tea and she asked me how I was doing. My friend had been divorced years earlier and knew the heartache and loneliness of formerly being a wife and then wrestling to adjust to altered circumstances. The hasty answer that came out of my mouth surprised me but did not surprise her. I, who had thought I had all my identity ducks in a row, replied that I was trying to figure out who I now was. She nodded knowingly, but I sat silent for a minute or two wondering if I still had my wits intact. What did I just say? My understanding of my identity was being pummeled by my emotions.

I battled for months in the strength of the Holy Spirit to keep a firm hold on my identity in Christ. How we see God—what we understand about him—is essential to every aspect of our lives. From those beliefs flows our understanding of ourselves. The more accurate our beliefs about God, the more our lives will be honoring to him (see John 10:28–29). I needed to remind myself of who God is and who I am in relation to him. This is the key relationship in life. I can lose everyone and everything, but I cannot lose God. He has hold of me and will not let me go. The last part of verse 5 in Hebrews 13 says, "I will never leave you nor forsake you." In the original language the verse has more the sense of "I will never not ever no never forsake you." God is telling us in the clearest possible way that he will never abandon his children.

Elisabeth Elliot, who was widowed twice, would open her radio program with the words, "You are loved with an everlasting love and underneath are the everlasting arms." Those lovely and comforting words come directly from Scripture: "I have loved you with an everlasting love; therefore I have continued my faithfulness to you" (Jer. 31:3) and "The eternal God is your dwelling place, and underneath are the everlasting arms" (Deut. 33:27). Everlasting, eternal, never ceasing, unending—he will never forget you, abandon you, leave you alone, ignore you, or reject you. Let these promises of God soak into your spirit until they revive your wilting soul.

I can't emphasize enough the importance of pursuing God with your whole heart especially now that you are a widow. It would be foolish to depend on other sources of comfort. Nothing can take the place of knowing who you are in Christ and leaning on God for all you need. Let's look at some portions of Scripture that teach us about God's care for widows.

THE BIBLE SPEAKS ABOUT WIDOWS

Running through most of the Bible verses regarding widows is one predominating theme—God's compassionate care for the relatively weak and vulnerable, particularly widows. This care is manifested in different forms. First, God is concerned that widows are treated with justice and kindness. "You shall not mistreat any widow or fatherless child" (Ex. 22:22). God wants widows to be assisted, comforted, and shown consideration. "[God] executes justice for the fatherless and the widow, and loves the sojourner, giving him food and clothing" (Deut. 10:18). God is our rock of refuge. Run to him with your cares and anxieties and cast them on him (see Ps. 46:1 and 1 Pet. 5:7). His unwavering love will hold you up. You have no cause for fear when the God of the universe has promised to make you his personal concern.

Second, God commands that widows be treated with compassion and charity:

> The Levite, because he has no portion or inheritance with you, and the sojourner, the fatherless, and the widow, who are within your towns, shall come and eat and be filled, that the LORD your God may bless you in all the work of your hands that you do. (Deut. 14:29)

Because God has special concern for widows, he requires that his people should also have that same concern. God is honored when his people imitate him by being helpful and kind to widows (see also Deut. 24:19–21; 26:12).

Third, God takes particular care of widows. Some of the most comforting verses in Scripture regarding widows are these:

> Father of the fatherless and protector of widows
>   is God in his holy habitation. (Ps. 68:5)

> The LORD watches over the sojourners;
>   he upholds the widow and the fatherless,
>   but the way of the wicked he brings to ruin. (Ps. 146:9)

> The LORD tears down the house of the proud
>   but maintains the widow's boundaries. (Prov. 15:25)

ADVICE TO WIDOWS

In 1 Corinthians 7 the apostle Paul gives advice to the church regarding *how to remain focused on the Lord without distraction* so that God's people could live in a way that would glorify him. How do we apply this counsel to our lives today? Let's pay particular attention to verses 39 and 40:

> A wife is bound to her husband as long as he lives. But if her husband dies, she is free to be married to whom she wishes, only in the Lord. Yet in my judgment she is happier if she remains as she is. And I think that I too have the Spirit of God.

Widows may remarry if they choose a husband who is a Christian. But what does Paul mean when he says that a widow is happier if she remains unmarried? He explains that the less worldly responsibility we shoulder, the more we can focus on Christ. By using the word "worldly" in verses 33 and 34, Paul does not mean that marriage is less honorable than singleness. Instead, he explains that marriage entails commitments and responsibilities that can distract a person from devotion to God.

Widows who remain single can direct their thoughts with less distraction onto the Lord, bringing them great happiness. It is permissible for them to remarry (a Christian man) and that could be a good thing. It can also be a good thing to remain a widow and be devoted to single-minded pursuit of Christ. This possibility for more concentrated devotion to the Lord is not because single people have more time, as has been suggested by some. The only way to reach that conclusion is by reading into the text an idea that is not there. The possibility for increased devotion comes not from having more time but from having less distraction, which marriage brings.

DEVOTION'S AMBITION

What is this devotion that Paul is talking about? What does it mean to be devoted to the Lord? Let's look at verses 32–35:

> I want you to be free from anxieties. The unmarried man is anxious about the things of the Lord, how to please the Lord. But the married man is anxious about worldly things, how to please his wife, and his interests are divided. And the unmarried or betrothed woman is anxious about the things of the Lord, how to be holy in body and spirit. But

the married woman is anxious about worldly things, how to please her husband. I say this for your own benefit, not to lay any restraint upon you, but to promote good order and *to secure your undivided devotion to the Lord.*

Devotion is a deep love and commitment. It is great dedication and loyalty to someone. "It is, of course, a characteristic of love that it is always thinking about the object of its love, and . . . that is true of every one of us."[3] Devotion entails having your mind preoccupied with the one you love. Undivided devotion to the Lord is tied to a gripping sense of who Christ is and what he has done for his people through his life, death, and resurrection. "Amazing love! How can it be that Thou, my God, shouldst die for me?"[4] "Love so amazing, so divine, demands my soul, my life, my all."[5] Sincere and fervent devotion to Christ involves both the inward glow of the soul and the outward flow of faithful service for him. It includes ardent love and affection and centering attention and activity on him.

From the backyard of my home, the view stretches for miles to the west. Sunsets are often spectacular with intense, glowing colors that rivet my attention. As the sun sets, the angle of the light produces a constant shifting of colors and patterns that delight the eye. Our devotion to Christ ought to be similar in producing a fixed and loving gaze on him. By seeking to be constantly aware of his presence, our hearts can be filled with warm, ardent, impassioned love for him. We will surely not be disappointed if we seek him with all of our being. He is unique—the God-man. He is perfectly human and perfectly divine. He is the radiance of God's glory (Heb. 1:3). How could we not be completely captivated by his matchless perfection and glory?

Over the last several years my responses to being widowed have varied. Whether at my worst or my best, God has been faithful beyond imagination. Early in my widowhood, I doubted that I would live long. I couldn't imagine enduring such pain for any length of time. But God strengthened my faith, and consequently I did not lose hope in him. His Spirit kept encouraging me through many means but primarily through his Word. God weeps with us over the death of our husband. We may feel that he is distant from us, but he is not. In his Word God says:

And be sure of this: I am with you always, even to the end of the age. (Matt. 28:20 NLT)

Yet he is actually not far from each one of us, for "in him we live and move and have our being"; as even some of your own poets have said, "for we are indeed his offspring." (Acts 17:27–28)

It is a wonderful testimony to the love and mercy of God that he has made it possible for believers in Christ to be admitted to heaven—a world of love. Marvel at the enormous love of God! He suffered the death of his only Son so that, among other blessings, we can grieve with hope. It is because God in his mercy enabled me to grieve with hope that you hold this book in your hands. God doesn't have favorites. He will help you too if you ask him.

> Be still, my soul: your God will undertake
> to guide the future as he has the past.
> Your hope, your confidence let nothing shake;
> all now mysterious shall be bright at last.
> Be still, my soul: the waves and winds still know
> his voice who ruled them while he dwelt below.[6]

3

TRUSTING GOD

Let your widows trust in me.

JEREMIAH 49:11

Several months after my husband died, a woman in a Bible study I was leading invited me to lunch at the retirement community where she lives. She is a widow whose husband died five years ago. I learn a lot from older Christian women, so I was delighted to spend some time with her. While we were enjoying the delicious food, I asked her how she had made it through the years since her husband died. She answered with two words: "Trust God." "I know that sounds simplistic," she added, "but that is how I did it."

SEEING THE INVISIBLE

Trust God. What would that look like for me as the days and months passed by? Trust God—with one of the hardest things ever to come into my life. I needed to learn to walk by faith, not by sight, in these circumstances and to trust God for everything just as my friend had. But my friend and I are quite different in the way we respond to life's crises. She has a straightforward way of accepting what comes into her life and dealing with it plainly and simply. I, on the other hand, seem constrained to analyze and dissect things. While her advice to trust God was just what I needed to hear, it left me with a lot of questions as to how to understand and implement that advice.

What does it mean to trust God? Trusting God involves depending upon him, relying upon him for all that we need both for body and soul. When we trust God, we put our full confidence in him. Trusting God means that we place our faith in him because he has promised his unfailing love and help. We believe that God will do what he says he will do. When we rely on God for everything, we show that we know him to be absolutely dependable. We can lean on him and he won't let us down. Some of the most precious words in all of Scripture for those who are suffering are found in 2 Corinthians 1:

> Blessed be the God and Father of our Lord Jesus Christ, the Father of mercies and God of all comfort, who comforts us in all our affliction, so that we may be able to comfort those who are in any affliction, with the comfort with which we ourselves are comforted by God. For as we share abundantly in Christ's sufferings, so through Christ we share abundantly in comfort too. (vv. 3–5)
>
> For we do not want you to be ignorant, brothers, of the affliction we experienced in Asia. For we were so utterly burdened beyond our strength that we despaired of life itself. Indeed, we felt that we had received the sentence of death. But that was to make us rely not on ourselves but on God who raises the dead. (vv. 8–9)

Verses 3 and 4 say that God is the Father of mercies and God of *all* comfort who comforts us in *all* our affliction. Tragedy forces us, whether we acknowledge it outwardly or not, to see how little of our lives we control. Once the funeral is over and we start living every day without our spouse, the future stretches out before us like an Iowa cornfield. Endless. God will be with us in those days with his loving comfort when we seek solace in him.

SEEING WITH THE EYES OF OUR SPIRIT

Probably the best known verse in all of Scripture regarding faith is Hebrews 11:1: "Now faith is the assurance of things hoped for, the conviction of things not seen." Another translation puts it this way: "What is faith? It is the confident assurance that what we hope for is going to happen. It is the evidence of things we cannot yet see." (NLT) God has given us the capacity in our soul to see and experience the invisible. Listen to what the apostle Peter said in 1 Peter 1:8–9:

> Though you have not seen [Christ], you love him. Though you do not now see him, you believe in him and rejoice with joy that is inexpressible

and filled with glory, obtaining the outcome of your faith, the salvation of your souls.

Verse eight says that we love Christ even though we have not seen him with our physical eyes. Christ rose from the dead and ascended into heaven. After this, the Lord provided for us another exactly like himself— the Spirit of Christ (see John 14:16–19). The Holy Spirit has been given to us, and we see him with eyes of faith. Like Moses, we can see him who is invisible (see Heb. 11:27).

The apostle Paul, writing to the Romans, said, "For his invisible attributes, namely, his eternal power and divine nature, have been clearly perceived, ever since the creation of the world, in the things that have been made. So they are without excuse" (Rom. 1:20). We see the evidence of God's existence in the creation. We see his divine power. To the Colossians Paul wrote, "[Christ] is the image of the invisible God, the firstborn of all creation" (Col. 1:15). And to Timothy, he wrote, "To the King of ages, immortal, invisible, the only God, be honor and glory forever and ever. Amen." (1 Tim. 1:17).

God is invisible to our physical eyes, but he is visible to the eyes of our spirit. He is real, trustworthy, faithful, and reliable. We need keen spiritual vision to see the Lord. In this regard I have benefited from Paul Tripp's teaching about imagination. He says that God's purpose in giving us imagination is to enable us "to relate to God who is a Spirit." Tripp's definition of imagination is that "it is not the ability to conjure up what is unreal, but the ability to see what is real but unseen. God gave us a spirit (our inner being) so we can relate to him who is a Spirit."[1] Tripp is not talking about fantasy but rather the ability to communicate with God, to relate to him Spirit to spirit.

Ask God to help you "see" him. You may want to pray this prayer attributed to Hudson Taylor: "Lord Jesus, make Yourself to me a living bright reality; more present to faith's vision keen than any outward object seen; more dear, more intimately nigh than e'en the sweetest earthly tie."[2] A. W. Pink makes this wise observation:

There are seasons in the lives of all when it is not easy, not even for Christians, to believe that God is faithful. Our faith is sorely tried, our eyes dimmed with tears, and we can no longer trace the outworking of His love.

Though you cannot now harmonize God's mysterious dealings with the avowals of His love, wait on Him for more light. In His own good time He will make it plain to you.[3]

Ask God to teach you how to rely on him for your well-being in every area of your life. We trust those we know and love. In order to trust God through this difficult time in life, we need to know him better.

Intimate knowledge of God comes through the Spirit ministering his Word to our spirits. God loves you. He pours out his love into your heart by his Holy Spirit (Rom. 5:5). Receive this love by faith. "He who did not spare his own Son but gave him up for us all, how will he not also with him graciously give us all things?" (Rom. 8:32). God understands your grief and the excruciating pain in your heart. His own dear Son suffered and died. Your heavenly Father knows the agony of loss. Trust him even when you cannot figure out why your circumstances are what they are. Humble yourself and believe the promises of God.

RUNNING TOWARD OR AWAY FROM GOD

If you've been a Christian for a number of years, it is likely you are familiar with Proverbs 3:5–6: "Trust in the LORD with all your heart, and do not lean on your own understanding. In all your ways acknowledge him, and he will make straight your paths." This promise has three conditions. You must: (1) have full confidence in the love God has for you; (2) recognize the finite limits of your own understanding and do not rely on it; and (3) pursue fellowship with God—know him in each and every circumstance.[4] As you do this, God will make your paths straight by guiding you through all of life.

Since I became a widow, other recently widowed persons have talked to me about their experiences with loss. Those who turn to God and seek him fervently hearten me. Sadly, others seem indifferent to pursuing God in their new circumstances. They appear to be holding a grudge against God along with suspicions regarding his goodness and wisdom. They give the impression that they are leaning on their own understanding and not acknowledging God in all their ways.

It is distressing to observe someone running from God rather than toward him. When we turn our backs on God, we are left with only idols to worship. An idol is something we trust in other than God. For the widowed person, the idol might be a replacement spouse, or alcohol, or the overuse of medication for anxiety and depression. What do I mean by a "replacement spouse"? This term describes a person to whom the widow attaches herself in an effort to fill the role formerly held by her spouse. Desperate to fill the void, the widow seizes control (so to speak) instead of praying and waiting on God. The replacement spouse is more an object than a subject, more desired for what he can do for the grieving one than for who he actually is.

LEANING ON GOD

Satan wants us to run from God and be hardened in our hearts toward him. However, if you trust God even when you don't understand what he is doing in your life, God is honored and pleased with your faith in him.

> And those who know your name put their trust in you,
>> for you, O LORD, have not forsaken those who seek you. (Ps. 9:10)

> Trust in him at all times, O people;
>> pour out your heart before him;
>> God is a refuge for us. (Ps. 62:8)

> It is better to take refuge in the LORD
>> than to trust in man. (Ps. 118:8)

> We know how much God loves us, and we have put our trust in his love.
> God is love, and all who live in love live in God, and God lives in them.
> (1 John 4:16 NLT)

Let's look at some additional Scripture verses that reinforce our trust in God. "The LORD is a stronghold for the oppressed, a stronghold in times of trouble. And those who know your name put their trust in you, for you, O LORD, have not forsaken those who seek you" (Ps. 9:9–10). The Bible is very clear regarding the special concern that God has for widows. In Bible times, a widow was cast onto the mercy of her family or the synagogue/church. If these sources failed her, she faced possible homelessness and starvation. "[God] executes justice for the fatherless and the widow, and loves the sojourner, giving him food and clothing" (Deut. 10:18). As you read in the Scriptures about the compassionate care of God for widows, let it shine a spotlight on the immense goodness of God. This display of God's character should produce a groundswell of love for him in your heart.

In the lobbing back and forth of accusations between Job and his friends, maltreatment of widows is mentioned: Eliphaz accuses Job, "You have sent widows away empty, and the arms of the fatherless were crushed" (Job 22:9). Job defends his actions in contrast to those of evildoers:

> They drive away the donkey of the fatherless;
>   they take the widow's ox for a pledge. . . .
> They wrong the barren, childless woman,
>   and do no good to the widow. (24:3, 21)

> If I have withheld anything that the poor desired,
>   or have caused the eyes of the widow to fail, . . .
> (for from my youth the fatherless grew up with me as with a father,
>   and from my mother's womb I guided the widow), . . .
> then let my shoulder blade fall from my shoulder. (31:16, 18, 22)

It's like trying to describe the worst deed you can think of to accuse someone of wrongdoing—"You weren't even kind to widows!" The assumption was that any godly person would display goodwill to widows. James makes it a test of true devotion to God:

> Religion that is pure and undefiled before God, the Father, is this: to visit orphans and widows in their affliction, and to keep oneself unstained from the world. (James 1:27)

In his love and concern for widows, God commands that widows be treated well.

KEEP YOUR EYES ON THE LORD IN LOVING TRUST

One of the most instructive portions of Scripture about trusting God is Isaiah 26:3–4: "You keep him in perfect peace whose mind is stayed on you, because he trusts in you. Trust in the LORD forever, for the LORD GOD is an everlasting rock." *The key to peace in the overwhelming grief of the loss of your husband is to keep your mind set on the Lord.* Loving God with deep affection is a powerful motivator for steering your thoughts onto him continuously. What we love preoccupies our minds. Ask God to give you grace to increase your love for him and power to keep your thoughts on him. You will need to read, study, and meditate on God's Word so that you grow in knowledge of him. You are probably thinking that it is impossible in your grief to concentrate on Scripture. In chapter 6 I have provided ways for you to profit from God's Word even when you find it hard to focus your mind on anything.

Trusting God is closely tied to loving God. "Let me hear in the morning of your steadfast love, for in you I trust. Make me know the way I should go, for to you I lift up my soul" (Ps. 143:8). As God's love is lavished on you, give this love away lavishly to others. Real, pure, unselfish love is rare in this world. Let the love of Christ that is in you spill over into the lives of the people around you. Doing so honors God and fills your heart with joy. God loves you. Trust him.

> Be still, my soul: when dearest friends depart,
> and all is darkened in the vale of tears,
> then shall you better know his love, his heart,
> who comes to soothe your sorrow and your fears.
> Be still, my soul: your Jesus can repay
> from his own fullness all he takes away.[5]

CHERISHING CHRIST

*Peace be to the brothers, and love with faith, from God the Father and
the Lord Jesus Christ. Grace be with all who love our Lord Jesus Christ
with love incorruptible.*

EPHESIANS 6:23–24

It was the middle of June. The sun was bright, the air hot and humid. The church, built in the late 1700s, was filled with family and friends. Strains of Handel's "Aria in F Major" filled the sanctuary as my father and I started down the aisle. Soon I heard myself saying, "I, Carol, take you, Roland, to be my wedded husband, to have and to hold from this day forward, for better for worse, for richer for poorer, in sickness and in health, to love and to cherish, till death us do part." Almost four decades later I said to myself, "We made it." By the grace of God we made it to the end. To the glory of God, we made it till death parted us.

EARTHLY AND HEAVENLY HUSBANDS

Loving husbands and wives cherish their marriages. When those marriages are ended by death, the surviving spouse can praise God for his goodness in having kept them together. Memories from all those years are cherished. Loving someone involves the act of caring as well as feelings, which is clear when we consider the synonyms for the word *love*: to treasure, value, prize, appreciate, relish, take pleasure in, revere, and attach importance to. As wonderful as marriage is, it is but a picture of something far greater and far more to be cherished:

> For no one ever hated his own flesh, but nourishes and cherishes it,
> just as Christ does the church, because we are members of his body.

> "Therefore a man shall leave his father and mother and hold fast to his wife, and the two shall become one flesh." This mystery is profound, and I am saying that it refers to Christ and the church. (Eph. 5:29–32)

The church universal (all believers everywhere from all times) is the body of Christ and the bride of Christ. As his body and bride, Christ cherishes the church by lovingly caring for it. This care exercised in love is manifested collectively and individually. Christ lovingly cares for the church as a whole and each Christian as an individual part of his body and bride.

So, what does Christ's cherishing of his church mean for Christian widows? It means that Christ is now taking care of us directly without the mediating presence of a husband. The Lord will use means such as our church family, his Word, and so on, but we remain his direct concern. There is a sense in which Christ is now our husband, but we need to understand this truth carefully. This is not some silly, romance-novel idea.

The Bible uses many metaphors to communicate truth. A metaphor is the application of a representative word or phrase to somebody or something to make a comparison. Christ as husband means that Christ is concerned to perform the duties of a husband to his wife in the areas of protection and provision and even in some aspects of companionship.

CHRIST AS FRIEND

If you are a Christian, Jesus has declared that he is your friend. Actually, he is your best friend. He is always faithful, always loving—perfect in every way.

> Greater love has no one than this, that someone lay down his life for his friends. You are my friends if you do what I command you. No longer do I call you servants, for the servant does not know what his master is doing; but I have called you friends, for all that I have heard from my Father I have made known to you. (John 15:13–15)

Christ laid down his life for his friends, his people. I've observed my earthly friends doing everything they could to help me through the loss of my husband, yet there are things that no earthly friend can ever provide when a husband is gone. Christ is the friend who can provide those things—peace, contentment, constant companionship, and assurance of never being left alone.

Charles Bridges in his commentary on Proverbs speaks of the friendship of Christ this way:

> Such is the sympathy of His love—*born for adversity*; so joined to us—the Friend and Brother we need; never nearer to us than when He is with us in our lowest depths of trouble; and, even though He is now our glorified Brother in heaven, yet He can still "sympathize with our weaknesses," still afflicted "in all our affliction"; presenting us to his Father, as His own elect, the purchase of His blood, the "members of His body." . . . Here is sympathy in all its fullness, and all its helpfulness. Here indeed is a *Brother born for adversity*.[1]

You are not alone. Christ, the Lord of the universe, is your friend. Stick close to him, cling to your friend. He will never reject you; he will never die and leave you all alone. He is all in all and the lover of your soul.

CLINGING TO CHRIST

The key to contentedly enduring the loss of your spouse is to cling to Christ. My granddaughter Emma clings to me when she wants to show her affection. Her clinging pictures how I should cling to Christ—a strong and determined holding on. It is a closeness that leaves no room for anything to come between. As Joshua summoned the Israelites to take possession of their land, he spoke these words:

> Only be very careful to observe the commandment and the law that Moses the servant of the LORD commanded you, to love the LORD your God, and to walk in all his ways and to keep his commandments and to *cling* to him and to serve him with all your heart and with all your soul." (Josh. 22:5)

In chapter 23, verse 8, Joshua says, "But you shall *cling* to the LORD your God just as you have done to this day." In verse 11 he adds, "Be very careful, therefore, to love the LORD your God."

THE UNDISTRACTED WIDOW

The Lord enables us to hold fast to him, or we would lose our grasp. He gives us the desire to cling to him and the strength and perseverance to hold on. Is this evident in your relationship with Jesus Christ? Do you cling to him because you love him dearly? Do you cling to him because you know that he first loved you and gave himself for you? He gives you every reason to cling and no reason to turn away. Do you desire Christ above everything else? Is he your greatest treasure and your greatest pleasure?

When David was in the wilderness of Judah he wrote Psalm 63. This psalm is particularly instructive for widows. David's wilderness was in Judah; the widow's wilderness is in her soul. Bereft of her husband, a widow needs to set her thoughts on the Lord and cherish him with her whole being. Here are David's loving words to God (between the verses, I have inserted thoughts that bring this beautiful love song home to the heart of a widow):

> O God, you are my God; earnestly I seek you;
> > my soul thirsts for you;
> my flesh faints for you,
> > as in a dry and weary land where there is no water. (v. 1)

O God, you are my God too. I need you, so I look for you because I will faint without your loving support. I've never before been in such a lonely, desolate situation. You continue to give me longings for you. How kind of you, Lord, to teach me to long for you and not for anything less. I know that only you are enough to satisfy my longings, because in the past you have been faithful to let me suffer and learn from my sinful longings.

> So I have looked upon you in the sanctuary,
> > beholding your power and glory. (v. 2)

You have taught me to gaze upon you, Lord. You have taken my face between your hands and redirected my attention—like a loving parent with a little child. When I see you rightly, I see your immense power and your great glory. Seeing you as you are strengthens my heart. I don't need to worry. You are powerful to protect me. You are glorious and worthy of my praise.

Because your steadfast love is better than life,
    my lips will praise you. (v. 3)

I praise you with my whole heart for who you are and for how you have steadfastly shown love to me. You know what I am feeling in my grief. You suffered the loss of your one and only Son so that sinners like me could know your love. You have not left me alone. I am not desolate. I am not without someone who loves me, for I have your love—the truest most steadfast love ever.

So I will bless you as long as I live;
    in your name I will lift up my hands. (v. 4)

As long as I live, may I praise you and speak well of you—especially in my grief. I will lift up my hands to you in praise. I will make music in my heart to you. I will lift up my soul to you, for you have proved your love and faithfulness.

My soul will be satisfied as with fat and rich food,
    and my mouth will praise you with joyful lips,
when I remember you upon my bed,
    and meditate on you in the watches of the night. (vv. 5–6)

O Lord, I pray that I will be satisfied in you alone.[2] Give me grace to praise you with great joy even though my heart is breaking from the loss of my husband. Thank you that many nights when I could not sleep because I was agitated from grief you gave me the ability to set my thoughts on you and to be at peace.

For you have been my help,
    and in the shadow of your wings I will sing for joy. (v. 7)

You have indeed been my help. If it weren't for your tender loving-kindness, I would have done something foolish or desperate because I am lonely and sad. I will sing for joy because I belong to you. In the midst of the deepest sorrow, you give me songs to sing—happy songs that sing your praises. Joy and sorrow mingle—I am becoming accustomed to it.

> My soul clings to you;
>   your right hand upholds me. (v. 8)

My soul holds tightly to you; it follows after you with intensity, for clinging is a result of cherishing. I am thankful for your nearness, for the gracious gift of your presence with me. Your powerful right hand won't let go of me. It is the foundation of my confidence. You will bring me through this valley of grief, and when I emerge, may I be more like you.

> But those who seek to destroy my life
>   shall go down into the depths of the earth;
> they shall be given over to the power of the sword;
>   they shall be a portion for jackals.
> But the king shall rejoice in God;
>   all who swear by him shall exult,
>   for the mouths of liars will be stopped. (vv. 9–11)

I have enemies, Lord—seen and unseen. Some doubt my words of praise for you and explain them away. In this psychologized culture, I am accused of being in denial. I am admonished for not being angry at you or at my deceased husband. Other enemies are of the dark presence. They would rejoice to see me waste away in my grief. But your power is seen clearly in my weakness. Like King David in the wilderness, I rejoice in your strength exercised on my behalf. My enemies will not triumph over me as long as you are my deliverer.

CHRIST'S AMAZING LOVE

The apostle Paul prayed for believers that Christ might dwell in their hearts through faith. He wanted them to know the vastness of Christ's love for his people. And so he prayed,

> For this reason I bow my knees before the Father, from whom every
> family in heaven and on earth is named, that according to the riches

of his glory he may grant you to be strengthened with power through his Spirit in your inner being, so that Christ may dwell in your hearts through faith—that you, being rooted and grounded in love, may have strength to comprehend with all the saints what is the breadth and length and height and depth, and to know the love of Christ that surpasses knowledge, that you may be filled with all the fullness of God. Now to him who is able to do far more abundantly than all that we ask or think, according to the power at work within us, to him be glory in the church and in Christ Jesus throughout all generations, forever and ever. Amen. (Eph. 3:14–21)

When we know this great love of Christ, we experience the fullness of God. Our souls are not empty, though in our grief we may feel that way. We cannot cherish Christ unless by the Holy Spirit's power we choose to put him first in our life—first before ourselves and before everyone else.

CHERISHING CHRIST AS OUR TREASURE

"The kingdom of heaven is like treasure hidden in a field, which a man found and covered up. Then in his joy he goes and sells all that he has and buys that field" (Matt. 13:44). In the loss of your husband, are you focusing your thinking on the treasure you can never lose? Your salvation in Jesus Christ is secure—you cannot lose him. You cannot be separated from him. He is your glorious inheritance. "This is eternal life, that they know you the only true God, and Jesus Christ whom you have sent" (John 17:3). "For God, who said, 'Let light shine out of darkness,' has shone in our hearts to give the light of the knowledge of the glory of God in the face of Jesus Christ" (2 Cor. 4:6). In his book *Holiness*, J. C. Ryle writes:

> The man whose soul is "growing" finds more in Christ to rest upon every year, and rejoices more that he has such a Saviour. No doubt he saw much in Him when first he believed. His faith laid hold on the atonement of Christ and gave him hope. But as he grows in grace he sees a thousand things in Christ of which at first he never dreamed. His love and power, His heart and His intentions, His offices as Substitute, Intercessor, Priest, Advocate, Physician, Shepherd, and Friend, unfold themselves to a growing soul in an unspeakable manner. In short, he

43

discovers a suitableness in Christ to the wants of his soul, of which the half was once not known to him.[3]

Christ is a treasure trove of delights. In him, we find the epitome of innumerable endearing qualities:

> He is the image of the invisible God, the firstborn of all creation. For by him all things were created, in heaven and on earth, visible and invisible, whether thrones or dominions or rulers or authorities—all things were created through him and for him. And he is before all things, and in him all things hold together. And he is the head of the body, the church. He is the beginning, the firstborn from the dead, that in everything he might be preeminent. For in him all the fullness of God was pleased to dwell, and through him to reconcile to himself all things, whether on earth or in heaven, making peace by the blood of his cross. (Col. 1:15–20)

What we delight in, we treasure. Delight yourself in Christ.

THE UNSEARCHABLE RICHES OF CHRIST

"To me [Paul], though I am the very least of all the saints, this grace was given, to preach to the Gentiles the unsearchable riches of Christ" (Eph. 3:8). In his commentary on Ephesians, Martyn Lloyd-Jones observes:

> Read through the epistles of Paul and note down on paper every reference he makes to Christ, to the Lord Jesus Christ, to Christ Jesus my Lord, and so on. It is quite astounding and amazing. As someone once put it, he was a "Christ-intoxicated" man. It is not surprising that he says, "To me to live is Christ"—Christ was the beginning, end, centre, soul, everything! His central message was that everything that God has for man is in Christ, and nowhere else. So we find him writing in his epistle to the Colossians these words: "In whom (Christ) are hid all the treasures of wisdom and knowledge" (2:3). It is all in Christ; and it is nowhere else.[4]

We widows need to focus on the cross of Christ. We must do so to honor God and, as C. J. Mahaney says, "for creating and sustaining our joy and our fruitfulness."[5] Keep Christ and his work on the cross as the central focus of your life. Concentrate on the wonders of Jesus Christ crucified and on the love and grace of God. Our salvation is a miracle. We deserve God's judgment, not God's grace. The cross of Christ should ignite and continually kindle our passion for him. Cherish Christ.

Be still, my soul: the hour is hastening on
When we shall be forever with the Lord,
When disappointment, grief and fear are gone,
Sorrow forgot, love's purest joys restored.
Be still, my soul: when change and tears are past
All safe and blessed we shall meet at last.[6]

5

ENJOYING THE HOLY SPIRIT

The grace of the Lord Jesus Christ and the love of God and the
fellowship of the Holy Spirit be with you all.

2 CORINTHIANS 13:14

It was a cold winter day and I was looking for a mindless task to fill up an afternoon. For many weeks I'd been working on matters regarding my husband's estate. I needed a change of pace. "Okay," I said to myself, "I'll clean a closet." But the closet most in need of cleaning was the one my heart couldn't yet face. I wasn't sure which would be worse: to continue seeing the clothes in my husband's closet or to see it empty. On that day, I pulled out a few pieces of his clothing and readied them to give away. Little by little over the next few months as the closet grew empty my heart was increasingly consoled and filled by the presence of the Spirit of Christ.

ENJOYING THE SPIRIT'S FULLNESS

In a collection of Puritan prayers we find these words: "O Holy Spirit, as the sun is full of light, the ocean full of water, heaven full of glory, so may my heart be full of You."[1] Pray that God will strengthen you through his Spirit in your inner being so that you will know the love of Christ for you in all its wonderful fullness. Knowing the depth of Christ's love for you instills increased love for him in your heart. Through his love, the Spirit relieves the pain of loss by creating a contentment that can produce intense delight as you receive Christ's love and as you love him in return.

> But now, O Israel, the LORD who created you says: "Do not be afraid, for
> I have ransomed you. I have called you by name; you are mine. When

you go through deep waters and great trouble, I will be with you. When you go through rivers of difficulty, you will not drown! When you walk through the fire of oppression, you will not be burned up; the flames will not consume you. For I am the LORD, your God, the Holy One of Israel, your Savior. I gave Egypt, Ethiopia, and Seba as a ransom for your freedom. Others died that you might live. I traded their lives for yours because you are precious to me. You are honored, and I love you. (Isa. 43:1–4 NLT).

Don't be afraid, for God has ransomed you, called you by name. When you and I are in deep waters and great trouble, he promises that he is with us. The death of my husband was certainly deep water for me. Rivers of difficulty—yes. Fire and flames—yes, yes.

My sorrow would have consumed me if it had not been for the consoling presence of the Spirit of God. In verse 4 the Lord says that you are honored and that he loves you! Those are astonishing words! God declares his love for us and calls us precious. He has set his love upon us not because we are worthy but because his nature is to love.

ENJOYING THE SPIRIT IN THE CREATION

"In the beginning, God created the heavens and the earth. The earth was without form and void, and darkness was over the face of the deep. And the Spirit of God was hovering over the face of the waters" (Gen. 1:1–2). Most days I walk along the road on which I live past meadows and fields where I see deer, foxes, birds, and various other wild creatures. These animals are gifts of God whose beauty brings me joy. Before God opened my eyes and gave me spiritual sight, I did not see evidence of him in the creation, although it was clearly there to see.

The reason I was blind to the work of the Spirit of God was that my spirit was dead. I was an unbeliever. "You, however, are not in the flesh but in the Spirit, if in fact the Spirit of God dwells in you. Anyone who does not have the Spirit of Christ does not belong to him" (Rom. 8:9). God in his great mercy, however, made me alive in Christ and gave me his Spirit to dwell in me as he does for every believer. He gave me the eyes of faith to see him and to see how he works in the world. The Spirit displays his work in macro (the night sky and the oceans) and in micro (tiny wildflowers and ladybugs).

Many times over the last several years, the Spirit of God has soothed the pain in my heart through the beauty of his creation. Perhaps your heart can be lifted above some of its pain as you observe God's handiwork in nature. Pray for eyes to see what God has done. Take a walk in a scenic place, plan a picnic with a friend or your children or grandchildren, sit by a window and enjoy the view, hike in the mountains, go to a zoological garden, or join a nature club. There are many ways to enjoy what God has created. "The heavens tell of the glory of God. The skies display his marvelous craftsmanship. Day after day they continue to speak; night after night they make him known" (Ps. 19:1–2 NLT). Pray that God's Spirit will open your eyes to the beauty around you and that it will soothe the ache in your soul.

As my relationship with the Lord deepened, I began to see more clearly the Spirit of Christ working in circumstances and people. Love outpoured and overflowing came to me during my husband's illness and death and beyond. The Spirit lavished love on me by varied means. It was easiest to see when it came through people. Oh, how it blessed me! God's love surprised me in so many ways and still does.

ENJOYING THE SPIRIT IN HIS IMAGE-BEARERS

Because human beings are made in the image of God, we can see God's glory in them. When we are grieving the loss of a spouse, the Holy Spirit moves in the hearts of people, and they become the couriers of his love. I see his glory in the deep-blue eyes of my grandchildren, in their sweet smiles, and wet kisses. Commenting on Psalm 112:4 Charles Spurgeon says, "We are at best but humble copies of the great original; still we are copies, and because we are so we praise the Lord, who hath created us anew in Christ Jesus." Make an effort to be a good observer of people. Look for the ways in which they reveal the image of God.

You might want to try an exercise that I did in order to understand this more clearly. Take a large piece of unlined paper and put a circle in the middle (see the diagram Seeing God in His Image-bearers). Then draw lines from that center hub and make spokes like in a wheel with a circle at each end. Label the center circle "Mirrors of Christ." Then in the surrounding circles put the name and attributes of a person who has been or is now in your life and who reflects aspects of Christ. For example, in one of the circles I put the name of my grandmother and then the words "cheerful," "loving," and "self-sacrificing," since she lived out before me those godly attributes. In another circle I put the name of a friend and the words "compassionate," "thoughtful," "dependable," "helpful," and "kind." These living mirrors are what they are by the grace of God. In these people, we see the image of God and it helps us to know him better.

SEEING GOD IN HIS IMAGE-BEARERS

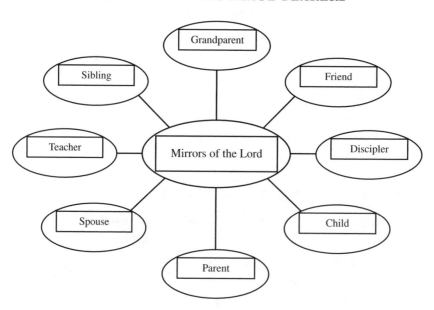

ENJOYING THE SPIRIT'S LOVING APPROACHES

Watch for God approaching you in love. Look diligently for him and pray for awareness of his presence, and the Holy Spirit will open your eyes to see ways in which Jesus Christ is indeed the lover of your soul. Watch for how he is protecting you and providing for you. You will be blessed if you pray and ask God to help you see him at work in small and large ways in your life. I find the seemingly small ways of God especially delightful. In them, only God and I know the details. It is an intimate and sweet way to see his love. It is akin to the secrets of lovers—heart knit to heart in sharing something no one else knows about.

When you realize that the God of the universe is personally connected to you and that he involves himself in what might seem to anyone else as an insignificant or routine event, then your heart overflows with delight in him. This love of God comes to us through the Holy Spirit.

> Therefore, since we have been justified by faith, we have peace with God through our Lord Jesus Christ. Through him we have also obtained access by faith into this grace in which we stand, and we rejoice in hope of the glory of God. More than that, we rejoice in our sufferings, knowing that suffering produces endurance, and endurance produces character, and character produces hope, and hope does not put us to shame, because God's love has been poured into our hearts through the Holy Spirit who has been given to us. (Rom. 5:1–5)

God's love has been poured out into our hearts through the Holy Spirit who has been given to us. Think about that—poured out! Not a trickle, not a few drops, but lavished on us in a downpour of love.

ENJOYING THE SPIRIT OF CHRIST

What treasures we receive through the Holy Spirit our helper and comforter! Only the powerful, sweet unfailing love of the Spirit of Christ could fill up the aching, yearning void of a heart that has been torn in two by the death of a beloved spouse. Mark Johnston helps us to understand the ministry of the Holy Spirit when he says, "So it dawned on the disciples when the Spirit came that the very One who had been Jesus' best friend and sustainer during his earthly life and ministry was to be their best friend and sustainer as well!"[2]

The Spirit imparts to us in our loneliness the presence of Christ. He fills up the void. Our experience of this filling is not immediate. As we grow closer to Christ, we are able to enjoy his presence more and more. We sense Christ's presence and commune with him through the Spirit who indwells us.

I enjoy caring for houseplants. The live greenery brings the outdoors inside and makes the house cheerful. Plants differ in their watering requirements, and a few are finicky. Some like to be drenched and then left to dry; others like more frequent watering of lesser amounts. If a plant loses turgor, it gets limp and hangs over the edge of its pot. When things get busy around here, I start to notice numbers of plants losing their turgor because I've neglected to water them. When I neglect to attend to the presence of the Spirit of Christ in my life, I lose spiritual turgor and hang over the edge of life limp and ineffective.

As Christians, we need a constant infusion of the Spirit's power in order to experience the comforting presence of Christ. In this way we honor God and are able to serve others to his glory. In the Gospel of John, chapter 15, Jesus used a botanical metaphor to get this point across to his disciples.

> I am the vine; you are the branches. Whoever abides in me and I in him, he it is that bears much fruit, for apart from me you can do nothing. . . . As the Father has loved me, so have I loved you. Abide in my love. . . . These things I have spoken to you, that my joy may be in you, and that your joy may be full. (John 15:5, 9, 11)

Speaking of the work of the Holy Spirit, Spurgeon says:

> The Holy Spirit consoles, but Christ is the consolation. If we may use the figure, the Holy Spirit is the Physician, but Jesus is the medicine. . . . If one is the Comforter, the other is the Comfort. Now, with such rich provision for his need, why should the Christian be sad and hopeless?[3]

Ask the Lord for grace to enjoy the Spirit and his work in your life. The Holy Spirit is your helper so that you can know and rejoice in the Lord always. "Rejoice always, pray without ceasing, give thanks in all circumstances; for this is the will of God in Christ Jesus for you. Do not quench the Spirit" (1 Thess. 5:16–19). Don't stifle or suppress the work of the Spirit in your life by failing to be thankful, to pray, and, yes, to rejoice in the Lord at all times.

ENJOYING THE COMPANIONSHIP OF THE SPIRIT

Remember that God the Father and God the Son have sent the Spirit to be in you and with you. You are not alone. You have not been abandoned although your feelings may insist that you are. Remind yourself of the truth. You belong to God, and he is providing all you need. When you need a friend to talk to, lift your voice and speak to the Spirit of Christ. He hears you. Don't rush to call a mere human being before seeking out the companionship and counsel of the One who can guide you perfectly and comfort you thoroughly.

The Spirit provides sufficient comfort especially through his Word, the Bible. In particular, read the Psalms and you will join the saints throughout the ages in being calmed and consoled by the Spirit who inspired the writers. Commenting on Psalm 63, James Boice points out that "David longs for God, and therefore David is satisfied with God. God does not hold himself back from those who seek him. Rather he gives himself to them fully and in increasingly fuller ways."[4] Seek him, and he will bless your longings for him.

Set your affection on Christ and enjoy him through the Holy Spirit. God is greatly honored when you do this, especially in the midst of your grief. Spurgeon observed that "when we see the bereaved widow overwhelmed in affliction yet having faith in Christ, oh! what honor it reflects on the gospel."[5] You and I can honor God by believing that he is with us in his Spirit and by finding joy in him that lifts our souls.

> Spirit of God, descend upon my heart;
> wean it from earth, through all its pulses move;
> stoop to my weakness, mighty as thou art,
> and make me love thee as I ought to love.
>
> Teach me to love thee as thine angels love,
> one holy passion filling all my frame;
> the baptism of the heav'n-descended Dove,
> my heart an altar, and thy love the flame.[6]

6

GAINING COMFORT FROM
GOD'S WORD

Your word is a lamp to my feet and a light to my path.
P S A L M   1 1 9 : 1 0 5

During the first long winter without my husband, I often found myself so fatigued that trying to read large portions of the Bible seemed impossible. I needed to find ways to study the Scriptures even when I couldn't concentrate. Holding up a large Bible was wearisome to me. My arms were quickly sapped of their strength. I was so exhausted from grief that I needed to devise other ways to read God's Word.

HOW TO APPROACH THE SCRIPTURES WHILE GRIEVING

The Bible software on my computer proved to be helpful. I printed out several pages of Scripture at one time selecting a large font and double spacing with large margins. I wrote my responses to God's Word between the lines. If you don't have Bible software, you can go online and print Scripture from a Web site that has different Bible versions available. If you don't have a computer, use a copier to enlarge several pages of Scripture. Then you can similarly write between or beside the lines. Using these methods helped me to make Scripture reading more physically comfortable and more personally applicable.

One of the sections of Scripture I studied was Paul's letter to the Philippians. Day after day, I read small portions, referenced other sources, and meditated through the letter verse by verse responding to the Scriptures and making personal application. If you are not sure where to find direction in the Scriptures, you might want to start with this letter. Paul's letter to the Philippians teaches us how to rejoice in the midst of suffering. His outlook is heavenward and his message is one of hope. Paul wrote to the Philippians while he was in prison in Rome. Keep this in mind as you read his letter and it will inspire you to respond to your situation in a godly way.

PERSONAL SCRIPTURE FLASH CARDS

Another method I used to keep my mind filled with God's Word was to make flash cards. Yes, big cards, similar to the ones we used for arithmetic in elementary school. I went to an office supply store and bought sheets of heavy paper scored to the size of postcards. Using my word processing program, I printed four portions of the Bible with different verses on each of the four card sections. The cards were easy to use at home or to pop into my purse and use wherever I was. Holding the cards was easy—even a fairly large stack of them.

After several weeks of looking at black ink on white cards, I decided to put pretty stickers on some of them, or I sketched on them with artist-quality colored pencils. I wanted them to be eye-catching, to make them a visually pleasant experience to read. The cards turned out to be a significant blessing to me. When I got anxious and couldn't sit still, I walked around the house with the cards reciting the words aloud. You might want to try making some for yourself or perhaps finding another way to keep Scripture in your mind so the Holy Spirit can use it to encourage and protect you.

It is often helpful to consult more than one version of the Bible. When I study Scripture, I like to compare versions in parallel fashion so I can see how the various translators interpret a verse. I use the English Standard Version as my foundational version and then compare it to the New American Standard Bible (1995), the New Living Translation (1996), and the New International Version. This method opens up more avenues for understanding the text. Use good judgment when choosing the versions from which you study. Many versions of the Bible are available, but not all of them are trustworthy.

In addition to putting Bible verses on cards, I also put some short quotes from Christian authors on flash cards. You can find rich teaching in the books listed in the suggested reading section at the end of this book. You might want to copy onto cards some statements that you find especially encouraging and edifying.

SKETCHING YOUR WAY TO COMFORT

Another way I motivated myself to read and memorize Scripture was to print onto beautiful computer paper verses that I wanted to include in my notebook. These were key verses that I needed to read over and over to make it through the day. I used different fonts and colored ink to make the pages a pleasure to look at. I played around with various font applications for eye appeal to etch the verses in my memory. God's Word strengthened me in my fight against my flesh and the Devil. I was tempted to let myself slide down into self-pity. Spiritual armor from the Word of God kept me standing firm in the Lord.

Another method I used to gain understanding, comfort, and strength from God's Word was to sketch a diagram of what a particular portion of Scripture was teaching me. You don't need to be an artist to utilize this method. Use artist's sketch paper and good-quality colored pencils or markers. You will have a more enjoyable experience if your materials are good quality.

When I was a seminary student, one of my systematic theology professors diagrammed concepts he was teaching by drawing "bean people." These figures were kidney-bean shaped, with faces, arms, and legs. His students will forever remember the beloved Mr. Robert Dunzweiler for his wise and faithful teaching that included his endearing bean people. If a learned and distinguished seminary professor can use bean people, you and I can use whatever we can draw to enhance our understanding of and comfort from God's Word. Don't be put off if your drawings aren't museum caliber. They are for your eyes only unless you want to use them as grown-up refrigerator art as I do. Ask God to teach you how to apply the Bible verses to your life as you sketch.

The process of making these resources was therapeutic for me. If you enjoy working with artist's tools and materials, you will find a sense of accomplishment in creating these cards, pages, and so on. Use whatever media and methods you enjoy. If you like photography, you might want to go out with your camera and record what you see of God in the creation. Then use your pictures along with Scripture and hymn texts to produce encouraging resources for yourself. If you like to sew, you might want to appliqué a wall hanging that reminds you of the faithfulness and care of God. The possibilities are numerous. Exercise your gifts and let them be a double blessing to you by honoring God and encouraging your heart.

PERSONALIZE YOUR HYMNBOOK

You might want to purchase a hymnbook for personal use.[1] If you aren't sure which hymnal to buy, ask your pastor for a recommendation. The theology in the words of hymns should be consistent with scriptural truth. Hymns are poems set to music. I use my hymnbook as a book of Christian poetry and am blessed by the expression of the poets. I found it exceedingly difficult to listen to music when I was newly widowed. Music speaks to our emotions, and mine were so raw that I couldn't bear to listen for long. It has taken me years to be able to sing without choking up, especially when I hear certain hymns or songs. But reading the words of the hymns was a powerful encouragement to me in those early days.

One of the reasons I included portions of hymn texts in this book is because beautiful poetry is so soothing to our souls. It says a lot with a minimum of words, which makes it memorable. It is easier for me when I am in a crisis to remember the words to hymns than to try to recall long sections of Scripture. Once I start singing or reciting the words to myself, the tune helps me along, and I can usually remember enough of the hymn to find comfort for my soul.

In addition to Bible verses, I printed hymn texts on patterned computer paper. Then I inserted these pages into my notebook. Whenever I needed encouragement to go on from day to day, I went to my notebook. It was a refreshing oasis for the eye and for the mind in the midst of a time that seemed black and empty. God used my notebook to keep me stable as the Spirit used his Word to renew my mind.

PRAYING THE SCRIPTURES

Grieving can make praying especially difficult. It is hard to concentrate, hard to know what to pray for, hard to stay awake, hard not to cry and get distracted. One of the most significant helps to me was praying Scripture aloud. I would choose a portion of Scripture and talk to my heavenly Father about it.

I found that it is especially helpful to pray the promises of God. Since a promise is an assurance that something will be done or not done, it is meant to give freedom from uncertainty or to overcome doubt. It is a declaration that inspires confidence. A promise is a guarantee, pledge, oath, or vow. Our ability to rest in a promise depends upon the person who is making or has made the promise. One of the reasons I wrote chapters about the person and work of God and put them near the beginning of this book is so that by knowing God better we can have confidence in his promises.

Because God is perfectly good, absolutely sovereign, and completely trustworthy, his Word and, in particular, his promises can inspire in us the greatest confidence. "Not one word of all the good promises that the LORD had made to the house of Israel had failed; all came to pass" (Josh. 21:45). "No distrust made [Abraham] waver concerning the promise of God, but he grew strong in his faith as he gave glory to God, fully convinced that God was able to do what he had promised" (Rom. 4:20–21). God kept his promises to the Israelites, and he will keep his promises to you and me. We can put our hope solidly in the promises of God. He cannot fail us. He is our solid rock.

When we are careful to pray the promises of God with a thankful, humble heart, we will find that trust grows as well as patience to wait God's timing. Apart from such humility and gratitude, we are likely to find ourselves demanding and impatient toward God. When you pray a promise of God, ask him to help you understand its meaning in its context within Scripture. Read the verses immediately preceding and following it to get a sense of how the words and ideas are being used. Read the whole chapter and the chapters before and after. If you need more insight, read the whole book in which the verse is imbedded. And, finally, be familiar enough with all of Scripture to know what God's purposes are in this world and what he is doing to bring them about.

If you find it difficult to weave Scripture into your prayers, ask for help from your pastor, Sunday school teacher, or other wise and knowledgeable Christians. Also, check the suggested reading list at the back of this book. You might want to use some psalms as I do in chapters 4, 9, and 11 and write between the verses.

BOOKS ABOUT GOD'S WORD

As you study God's Word, you will come across portions of Scripture that are not as clear to you as others. When you feel ready for deeper study, you can consult commentaries written by Bible scholars. Commentaries help explain the meaning of various texts. Just as it is important to use Bible translations that are reliable, it is important to use commentaries that are reliable. Two resources that can help you choose good commentaries are, for the Old Testament, Tremper Longman's *Old Testament Commentary Survey*, 2nd edition, and, for the New Testament, D. A. Carson's *New Testament Commentary Survey*, 4th edition. Each book gives an overview of the benefits and drawbacks of all the major commentaries on each book, rating them and recommending those that are most helpful.

You may be thinking that using commentaries is beyond what you can handle at this point. If so, that's understandable. But someday, you may want answers to thorny questions, and knowing about these resources may prove a valuable help to you. When grieving the loss of your spouse, you are in the University of Adversity. If you respond faithfully to God's work in your life at this time, he will teach you many things that will bless you. You will be able to help others in the future when they encounter similar trials. Be a diligent student so that you can serve God in his kingdom work.

> Break thou the bread of life, dear Lord, to me,
> as thou didst break the loaves beside the sea;
> throughout the sacred page I seek thee, Lord,
> my spirit pants for thee, O living Word.
>
> O send thy Spirit, Lord, now unto me,
> that he may touch my eyes and make me see;
> show me the truth concealed within thy Word,
> and in thy Book revealed I see the Lord.[2]

7

LEARNING FROM EXAMPLES OF BIBLICAL WIDOWS

As [Jesus] drew near to the gate of the town, behold, a man who had died
was being carried out, the only son of his mother, and she was a widow. . . .
And when the Lord saw her, he had compassion on her
and said to her, "Do not weep."

LUKE 7:12–13

They were married in their teens. Seven years later, he died leaving her all alone. She never remarried even though she lived a long life. We know of no children from their marriage nor do we know of any extended family members who might have been able to help her. She spent a lot of time fasting and praying. Her name is Anna.

FOLLOWING IN FAITHFUL FOOTSTEPS

In this chapter, we want to look at and learn from the lives of some of the widows mentioned in the Bible. Sometimes when we read the Scriptures, we experience difficulty identifying with the lives of the people we read about. They lived long ago, and the culture and times were different. We can turn, however, to knowledgeable Bible teachers for help in gleaning from God's Word both a faithful understanding of the text and application to our lives.

The stories in the Bible that describe the lives of individuals are not there by accident. One of the purposes of these stories is to give us examples of how to live or not to live our lives. These people are models of behavior from which we learn. If their attitudes and behavior were exemplary, we are encouraged to copy them. If not, we are warned to avoid modeling our lives after them. "Beloved, do not imitate evil but imitate good. Whoever does good is from God; whoever does evil has not seen God" (3 John 11).

KEEN OBSERVATIONS

One of the best ways to learn is from observing the way someone else does something. We learn what not to do from bad examples.

> Now these things took place as examples for us, that we might not desire evil as they did. . . . Now these things happened to them as an example, but they were written down for our instruction, on whom the end of the ages has come. (1 Cor. 10:6, 11)

We learn what we should do from good examples. Our foremost good example, of course, is the Lord Jesus Christ: "For I have given you an example, that you also should do just as I have done to you" (John 13:15). Throughout the Gospels, we read of Christ teaching his followers to do as he does. He gathered the twelve disciples around him so that day and night they could learn from his example as well as his words. We too need to imitate the Lord as well as those who walked faithfully with him:

> Therefore be imitators of God, as beloved children. (Eph. 5:1)
> And you became imitators of us and of the Lord, for you received the word in much affliction, with the joy of the Holy Spirit, so that you became an example to all the believers in Macedonia and in Achaia. For not only has the word of the Lord sounded forth from you in Macedonia and Achaia, but your faith in God has gone forth everywhere, so that we need not say anything. For they themselves report concerning us the kind of reception we had among you, and how you turned to God from idols to serve the living and true God, and to wait for his Son from heaven, whom he raised from the dead, Jesus who delivers us from the wrath to come. (1 Thess. 1:6–10)
> For God is not unjust so as to overlook your work and the love that you have shown for his name in serving the saints, as you still do. And we desire each one of you to show the same earnestness to have the full

assurance of hope until the end, so that you may not be sluggish, but imitators of those who through faith and patience inherit the promises. (Heb. 6:10–12)

Remember your leaders, those who spoke to you the word of God. Consider the outcome of their way of life, and imitate their faith. (Heb. 13:7)

The apostle Paul exhorted people in the churches to which he ministered to follow his own example: "Brothers, join in imitating me, and keep your eyes on those who walk according to the example you have in us" (Phil. 3:17). "I urge you, then, be imitators of me" (1 Cor. 4:16). "Be imitators of me, as I am of Christ" (1 Cor. 11:1).

SIX DECADES OF FAITHFUL SERVICE

God has preserved for us in his Word stories of the lives of some widows. My favorite story is that of Anna told by Luke in his Gospel. In chapter 2 we find three verses that specifically mention Anna:

And there was a prophetess, Anna, the daughter of Phanuel, of the tribe of Asher. She was advanced in years, having lived with her husband seven years from when she was a virgin, and then as a widow until she was eighty-four. She did not depart from the temple, worshiping with fasting and prayer night and day. And coming up at that very hour she began to give thanks to God and to speak of him to all who were waiting for the redemption of Jerusalem. (vv. 36–38)

Notice it says that Anna was a prophetess. This does not mean that she foretold the future or that she necessarily received direct revelation from God. A prophet can simply be a person who tells truth to others. Anna may have been a teacher of the Word of God, most likely to women who visited the temple. She worshiped God with fasting, prayer, and thanksgiving.

What else can be gleaned from this portion of Scripture regarding the widow Anna? John MacArthur, in his book *Twelve Extraordinary Women*, gathers many elements from biblical history that open up for us a wider picture of her life. He says it is likely that Anna lived on the temple grounds in one of the apartments in the outer courts:

Perhaps because of her long faithfulness, her obvious spiritual gifts, her steadfast devotion to the Lord, and her constant commitment to her ministry of prayer and fasting, temple officials had given her a small chamber. . . .

In any case, it was ultimately the Lord who had graciously provided her a place in His house and sovereignly orchestrated whatever arrangement she might have had with the temple custodians. . . .

She was singularly and completely devoted to the service and worship of God—mostly through her prayers and fasting. The manner of her praying, accompanied by fasting, speaks of her own self-denial and sincerity.[1]

On the day when Mary and Joseph brought Jesus to the temple, they encountered there a man who lived in Jerusalem whose name was Simeon. In Luke's Gospel, Luke describes Simeon as righteous and devout and waiting for the appearance of the Messiah. God had revealed to Simeon that he would not die until he had seen the Messiah. Full of the Holy Spirit, Simeon took Jesus in his arms and blessed God. MacArthur says it is likely that Simeon and Anna knew one another prior to the day that Jesus was brought into the temple.

Now, Herod's temple was a massive building, and the temple complex was huge, surrounded by a courtyard with thousands of people milling around at almost any given time. . . .

At that very instant, just while Simeon was blessing the child with inspired words of prophecy, the Spirit of God providentially led this elderly woman [Anna] to a place where she was within earshot. . . .

The Messiah had finally come, and Anna was one of the very first to know who He was. She could not keep that news to herself. She thus became one of the very first and most enduring witnesses of Christ.[2]

Anna is an exemplar of the undistracted widow. Here are some things we may imitate from her example:

- Devotion to God in public and private worship
- Service for God and others

- Fervent prayer
- Fasting
- A heart full of gratitude to God
- Faithful witness for God to all who will listen

We need to ask the Lord to give us hearts like Anna's that long to see him and serve him. Praise God that he has preserved in his Word the faithful example of Anna.

A MOTHER-IN-LAW STORY

Next, let's take a look at three widows whose story of widowhood is told in part in the Old Testament book of Ruth. Naomi and her family were from Bethlehem in Judah. Because there was a famine in the land, Naomi, her husband, and two sons left Judah to go to the land of Moab. While in Moab, Naomi's husband died and both of her sons married Moabite women. Ten years later, both sons died leaving their wives, Ruth and Orpah, as widows. Thus, Naomi found herself in a foreign country with no husband and no children. Her only family consisted of her two daughters-in-law, who were also childless.

Keep in mind that several themes run throughout the book of Ruth including the main theme of the Lord's work in the history of redemption. But for our purposes, we want to focus on the relationships among these three women. While we do not have much information, we can glean some important lessons from what we do have.

Upon hearing that Judah had recovered from the famine, Naomi decided to return there. As she set out, both of her daughters-in-law chose to go with her. "But Naomi said to her two daughters-in-law, 'Go, return each of you to her mother's house. May the LORD deal kindly with you, as you have dealt with the dead and with me'" (Ruth 1:8). Note that Naomi mentions their kindness to her. After saying this, Naomi kisses them, and they both weep openly. Here we have a description of loving relationships among these widows. Only godly character in Naomi could have elicited such a response from these younger women.

Both Orpah and Ruth declare their intent to return with Naomi to Judah, but Naomi persists in her counsel to them to go back to the homes of their parents and to marry again. Orpah decides to follow that counsel, kisses Naomi good-bye, and returns to her family of origin; however, Ruth does not. The Bible tells us that "Ruth clung to [Naomi]" (v. 14).

Once again, Naomi voices her advice to Ruth to go back to her people. Here is Ruth's beautiful and courageous reply:

> Do not urge me to leave you or to return from following you. For where you go I will go, and where you lodge I will lodge. Your people shall be my people, and your God my God. Where you die I will die, and there will I be buried. May the LORD do so to me and more also if anything but death parts me from you. (vv. 16–17)

From this exquisite testimony, it is clear that Ruth has come to know the true God through her mother-in-law, Naomi. What a wonderful influence the widowed Naomi had on her widowed daughter-in-law! That Ruth would make such a confession and then act on it is clearly due to the grace of God working through the faithfulness and love that she saw in Naomi.

You can read the rest of the story in the book of Ruth. But, for now, what can we learn from this portion of the story? In your widowhood, you can have a tremendously positive influence on others. Naomi must have shown deep love and care for her daughters-in-law or else they would not have considered leaving their homeland to go with her to a foreign nation. This kind of love requires keeping your own grief in perspective and ministering to the needs of those around you.

It is reasonable to assume that Naomi's response to the death of her husband was exemplary, because when her married sons died, their widows looked to Naomi for comfort and strength. We need to be aware of the trials of others and to comfort and help where we can, even if we are grieving. Loss is not an occasion for expecting or demanding exclusive attention from the people around us. Though grief may make us feel as though our hearts are being ripped in pieces, we can gain strength from the Spirit to reach out to others in the distresses of their lives.

THE WIDOW OF NAIN

In the story of a widow who lived in a town called Nain, we see a miracle performed:[3]

> Soon afterward [Jesus] went to a town called Nain, and his disciples and a great crowd went with him. As he drew near to the gate of the town, behold, a man who had died was being carried out, the only son of his mother, and she was a widow, and a considerable crowd from the town was with her. And when the Lord saw her, he had compassion on her and said to her, "Do not weep." Then he came up and touched the bier, and the bearers stood still. And he said, "Young man, I say to you, arise." And the dead man sat up and began to speak, and Jesus gave him to his mother. Fear seized them all, and they glorified God, saying, "A great prophet has arisen among us!" and "God has visited his people!" And this report about him spread through the whole of Judea and all the surrounding country. (Luke 7:11–17)

The miracle pointed to the fact that Jesus is the Messiah. People witnessed the mind-blowing event of seeing a dead person brought back to life. They recognized the presence of God's power among them in the person of Jesus.

Something else is happening in this event. We are told that Jesus had compassion on this widow. Her husband was dead and now her only son was dead also. She was in a most desolate state emotionally and probably also financially with no male family members to provide for her. Jesus had compassion on her. What does this mean? It means that he was sympathetic to her suffering and wanted to help her. And she received amazing help from him! Her son was raised from the dead and given back to her by the power of Jesus. This miracle provided a sign of his true identity and benefited the widow in her distress.

What can we learn from the story of the widow of Nain? We learn that Jesus has a special heart of compassion for widows. Though we cannot expect our dead to be raised (though God can choose to do that if he wills and surely will do it at the second coming of Christ), we may expect that our Lord still shows compassion for Christian widows. He will help us with sympathetic words and actions through his Spirit in the Word and other means to communicate this heartfelt sympathy to us. He does not leave us comfortless.

> For all the saints who from their labors rest,
> who thee by faith before the world confessed,
> thy name, O Jesus, be forever blest.
> Alleluia! Alleluia![4]

8

LEARNING FROM EXAMPLES OF CONTEMPORARY WIDOWS

Dear brothers and sisters, pattern your lives after mine,
and learn from those who follow our example.
PHILIPPIANS 3:17 (NLT)

Along with eight other widows, I was invited to lunch at the home of a friend who has been widowed for almost ten years. Half of the women invited were so busy with grandchildren and ministry involvement that we ended up a party of four. One of the women has been a widow for many years and is now in her eighties. Another, who is about a decade older than I, lost her husband almost exactly one year after my husband died.

FINDING WIDOWS TO FOLLOW

This little gathering was a time of significant encouragement for me. It was not quite a year since my husband's death when we all got together. In almost every way, these women gave me hope for the future. They are bright, active, and beautiful. They love the Lord and faithfully serve his church in varied ways. I've received from them sweet notes full of wise words, and they've called just when I needed to hear a friendly voice. Even though I am certain they would not claim to have done so, they mentored me by simply and consistently living out their lives in love with the Lord and with happy hearts to serve him. They were like a living road map for me as I sought to find my way to a place of stability during my first year of widowhood.

We can learn a lot of valuable lessons from widows who follow Christ. Observing their lives can be instructive and inspiring. Watching their courage and perseverance can strengthen us. Their examples help us feel less alone, less peculiar, less confused about how to go on in life without our husbands. Be a good observer of those who walk in step with the Holy Spirit displaying the glory of God in their conduct and attitudes.

THE LOVER'S DEATH

"The death of the beloved was the beloved's own death. . . . But the death of the beloved is also the lover's death, for it means, in a different but perhaps equally fearsome way, a going through the Valley of the Shadow."[1] I found these words in a little booklet by Elisabeth Elliot and read them over and over shortly after my husband died. They describe so perfectly how I felt inside—like a dark grotto of grief shadowed by death.

I first heard Elisabeth Elliot speak at a seminar. I had the privilege of hearing her speak again in chapel when I was a seminary student. I have read a number of her books and enjoyed listening to her radio program, "Gateway to Joy." These were the opening words to her program: "You are loved with an everlasting love and underneath are the everlasting arms. This is your friend, Elisabeth Elliot . . . " Not until the show terminated did I realize how much I missed hearing the truth of those opening words spoken in her steady, calm, reassuring voice. No matter how chaotic my life might be that day, Elisabeth's unruffled manner, which flowed from her trust in God, was a powerful example.

In the dark cavern of bereavement, I looked for a beacon to direct me. I read Scripture and was encouraged by its witness to God's care for widows. I also searched for other sources of solid Christian encouragement and found in Elisabeth's little booklet *Facing the Death of Someone You Love* an outline for how to endure in a godly way the death of my husband. On my bookshelf I have nine books written specifically for widows by widows, but none of them helped me like Elisabeth's booklet.

What made Elisabeth's counsel stand out from the rest? First and foremost, Elisabeth has lived all her life for God. She thinks from a biblical perspective and does not get sidetracked by cultural fads. Second, she has been widowed twice. How sobering it was for me to realize that she had gone through the pain of bereavement with the deaths of two husbands. Third, in her suffering she did not blame God or get angry at him but instead sought to honor him in the midst of her suffering. Lastly, though she acknowledged the emotional pain of bereavement, she did not wallow in it or use it as an excuse to sin. Here was a former widow whose example I could follow with confidence.

In the *Elisabeth Elliot Newsletter* of May/June 2000, Elisabeth responded to some mail she received with these words:

> Occasionally I am asked if I have ever been bitter or angry toward God because He took from me two much-loved husbands (He has mercifully given me yet a third—none of them sought after). Unless my memory completely forsakes me I believe I can honestly answer *no*. Our adversary the devil has tempted me in many ways, but I don't think anger at God is one of them.[2]

She goes on to list five reasons why she did not succumb to the sin of anger at God. If this is an area in which you are struggling, it will be very helpful for you to go online and read her thoughts. They run against the grain of the vast majority of grief counselors. Yet she is precisely right. If we want to think biblically about grieving, we will heed the wisdom of her words.

IS WIDOWHOOD A GIFT?

In her book *Loneliness*, Elisabeth wrote a chapter entitled "The Gift of Widowhood." Here is how she explains what that means:

> I had prayed as earnestly as a child and a teenager and a woman can pray, *Thy will be done*. The coming of this transcendent authority into one's life is bound to be an active thing, an immense disruption at times.
>
> This was one of those times. [God] had done more than merely "allow" a thing to "happen" *to* me. I do not know any more accurate way of putting it than to say that He had given me something. He had given me a gift—widowhood.
>
> How can I say such a thing?
>
> He does not whisk us at once to Glory. We go on living in a fractured world, suffering in one way or another the effects of sin—sometimes our

own, sometimes others'. Yet I have come to understand even suffering, through the transforming power of the Cross, as a gift, for in this broken world, *in* our sorrow, He gives us Himself; *in* our loneliness He comes to meet us, as in George Matheson's He came as the Love that would never let him go.

In His death Jesus Christ gave us life. The willingness of the Son of God to commit Himself into the hands of criminals became the greatest gift ever given—the Bread of the world, in mercy broken. Thus the worst thing that ever happened became the best thing that ever happened.

It can happen with us. At the Cross of Jesus our crosses are changed into gifts.

The Love that calls us into being, woos us to Himself, makes us His bride, lays down His life for us, and daily crowns us with lovingkindness and tender mercy, will *not*, no matter how it may appear in our loneliness, abandon us.[3]

Elisabeth Elliot is an example of a woman who, in two seasons of her life, was an undistracted widow. Author Patti Broderick counsels widows with these words:

> Those of us who are grieving face a real temptation to fill our voids with anything so that we do not feel the pain and the emptiness. We are vulnerable. But eating, drinking, carousing, sleeping, and taking exotic vacations will not fill the emptiness. In the end they only exacerbate the feelings of isolation and make us feel worse about ourselves. We have to choose to fill the void with a relationship with someone who is perfectly trustworthy with our vulnerabilities. God is real. He really can do everything He promises.[4]

These are wise and insightful words. We can trust God to do only good to us and for us. Turning first to God and seeking his comfort and friendship will honor him and bless us.

DEVELOP DISCERNMENT

Hundreds of books are available on the subject of widowhood from both a secular and a sacred perspective. If you choose to read secular books on widowhood and/or grieving, I urge you to use discernment as you read. Much of the advice given in them conflicts with the Scriptures. Keep in mind the admonition of Psalm 1:1–2:

> Blessed is the man
> who walks not in the counsel of the wicked,
> nor stands in the way of sinners,
> nor sits in the seat of scoffers;
> but his delight is in the law of the LORD,
> and on his law he meditates day and night.

Remember that the word *wicked* in the Psalms refers to any person who is not a believer in the Lord. Therefore, you must carefully examine the counsel given by a non-Christian.

Let me say a word about reading books on widowhood or spousal grief by Christian authors. You recall that in Acts 17 Paul and Silas were preaching in Asia Minor. The response of the believers in Berea is instructive and commendable:

> The brothers immediately sent Paul and Silas away by night to Berea, and when they arrived they went into the Jewish synagogue. Now these Jews were more noble than those in Thessalonica; they received the word with all eagerness, *examining the Scriptures daily to see if these things were so*. Many of them therefore believed, with not a few Greek women of high standing as well as men. But when the Jews from Thessalonica learned that the word of God was proclaimed by Paul at Berea also, they came there too, agitating and stirring up the crowds. (vv. 10–13)

It is not wise to read books by Christian authors (including this one) without comparing what is written to what is taught in God's Word. The fact that an author is a Christian does not necessarily mean that what is written is consistent with biblical teaching. Paul instructed the Philippians to be discerning:

> It is my prayer that your love may abound more and more, with knowledge and all discernment, so that you may approve what is excellent,

and so be pure and blameless for the day of Christ, filled with the fruit of righteousness that comes through Jesus Christ, to the glory and praise of God. (Phil. 1:9–11)

It is your responsibility to ask yourself whether what the author is teaching is true or false. I have endeavored in this book to do my best to teach what is true according to the Bible, but no book by any author is infallible other than the Holy Scriptures. If you need assistance with discerning what books are biblically reliable, ask your pastor for recommendations.[5]

Even though you may be weary and exhausted from grief, it is important to ask yourself whether what you are reading is biblically sound material. If you do not make this effort, you could be led astray even by a well-meaning Christian. As I read Christian books about widowhood, I found help in some but was unpleasantly surprised at the poor counsel given in others.

FROM MY MAILBOX

Widows with whom I am personally acquainted have been a source of delight and encouragement. They have ministered to me in all sorts of ways. Just below are excerpts from notes written by four of them. I hope that reading the words they wrote to me will encourage you.

> I want to express my deepest sympathy to you and your family. I have been where you are and I *know* how hard it is. My prayers are for you and your family, that God will comfort you and give you strength through the days ahead. It surely must be a blessing for Rolly to be relieved from his suffering, and while you will miss him so much, especially at this time of the year, just think how blessed he will be celebrating his first Christmas in heaven.

> No words can adequately express my heartfelt sympathy in your loss of Roland. This has been a long and hard year with much pain and sadness. I thank the Lord, Carol, for your faith and trust in your heavenly Father throughout the struggles, painful circumstances, and unanswered questions. You have sought to honor your heavenly Father and have been a testimony to others of God's grace in the hard times. My continued prayer is for the Lord's peace, strength, and comfort during this very

hard time. Tuesday's [funeral] service was a blessing and reflected your desire for others to know the Savior you love and serve. It was God-honoring, and I pray God may use it in the lives of others.

My thoughts and prayers and love are with you. I know what you are going through, and it hurts. May the Lord do in your life what only he can—strengthen you with his love, fill you with his assurance, bless you with his peace, and hold you in his arms, as I hold you in my prayers.

God is so kind to allow me to have these wonderful women as friends. I am not walking this path of widowhood alone. God is with me and so are these sisters in Christ.

Likewise, he is with you, dear widowed sister, and he wants to encourage you and uphold you partly through the widows in your life. You are not alone. May the God of all comfort and hope lift your heart and give you joy even in the midst of your grief. Breathe deeply, believe deeply, and follow in his footsteps. No matter how dark things look—and I know they can look impossibly dark—you are not alone in that darkness. Daylight is coming and with it joy.

THE WIDOWS IN YOUR LIFE

If it is awkward for you to approach a widow about your own loss, you might want to consider starting a conversation with some of the following questions:

- What did you find most helpful after your husband died?
- What parts of Scripture have been most comforting to you?
- How have you been able to keep going?
- What do you do during the holidays?
- What sort of opportunities do you have to serve your church?
- Are you part of a widows' group?

Most widows will be glad to help you by answering your questions. Just remember to be considerate.

Before you begin, inquire how she feels about being asked about her life as a widow. If she becomes teary-eyed, ask her if it is acceptable to continue with the conversation. Depending upon the length of time she has been widowed, her emotions may still be quite tender. Even some who have been widowed for several years or more can well up with tears. But just because she tears up doesn't necessarily mean she wants to end the conversation. Most widows are pleased when someone wants to know and talk about what they've been through and how they are doing. Sensing that they can be of help to you will give them a sense of satisfaction. Following up your conversation with a sweet note of thanks is a lovely gesture.

God displays his tender loving care in the lives of those who submit to him and trust that he will never fail them. Christian widows can inspire one another to face the future with confidence because they have a heavenly Father who has promised to protect them and to provide all they need.

> For the joy of human love, brother, sister, parent, child,
> friends on earth and friends above for all gentle thoughts and mild,
> Lord of all, to thee we raise this our hymn of grateful praise.[6]

GRIEVING IN A GODLY WAY

But we do not want you to be uninformed, brothers, about those who are asleep, that you may not grieve as others do who have no hope.

1 THESSALONIANS 4:13

I enjoy playing the game Scrabble. Though the dictionary of the English language is not on my list of recreational reading, I find it fascinating at times. I have six thesauri and at least a half dozen dictionaries. Words are my tools as a counselor, teacher, and author. But words fail us at times. When I started thinking about this chapter, I figured it would be a straight-forward presentation. Then I sat down to actually write it and realized how hard it is to convey in words the thoughts and feelings associated with grieving the death of a husband.

WHEN WORDS FAIL

In order to connect again to the feelings I had immediately after my husband died, I got out my personal journals from that time and started reading them. After a half hour I stopped, though I hadn't gotten through much I wanted to reread. Reading the journals had three effects on me: (1) it reminded me of how crushingly sad that time was; (2) it made me realize how far I have moved beyond those initial feelings; and (3) it made me more thankful than ever that my heavenly Father has enabled me to rest in him and to move on from those intense emotions.

Reading this chapter may feel like being without a coat on a cold day. The reason is that we live in a culture that promotes the belief that we all deserve to have life our way. It's hard not to absorb that message into our own thinking. Over the last several decades, a cultural shift has occurred in which we are influenced to live according to how we feel about things instead of how we think about things. Yet while we don't want to ignore how we feel, we do want to be careful not to be driven by our emotions. We want to think about our grief in a way consistent with God's Word and let our feelings derive from those thoughts.

PATTERNS IN GRIEVING

The way we grieve is influenced by many factors: our family background, our socioeconomic status, our level of education, our culture, and so on. Each woman grieves the loss of her husband differently and at her own pace. Grief does not occur in set stages.

> There is no biblical evidence to suggest that grief occurs in stages as is proposed by writers such as Elizabeth Kubler-Ross. Instead, grieving is more like the last weeks of winter in which you think the cold days are abating only to awaken the next morning to a layer of snow on the ground. Individual aspects of the experience of loss come and go and cycle back in on us again as we adjust to the ways our lives are changed by loss.[1]

Periods of intense grief become fewer and farther between as you learn to lean on God and adjust to your new circumstances.

I've observed three general patterns of response that widows display in grieving the death of their husbands:

- Stoicism—the Rock-of-Gibraltar widow
- Emotionalism—the let-it-all-hang-out widow
- Faithfulness—the resting-in-the-God-who-is-there widow

A stoic denies the reality of the situation and lives as if the loss does not touch her. In contrast, the widow who allows herself to be at the mercy of her emotions fails to control herself. I am not saying that it is wrong to pull yourself together in the strength of the Lord and contain your tears at times. Nor am I saying that it is wrong to shed tears of grief in the presence of others. Tears are appropriate at times, even years later. But the Bible calls us to honor God in everything we do (see 1 Cor. 10:31; Col. 3:17). God is not honored when we act super-Christian, as though grief cannot touch us, or sub-Christian, as though grief has robbed us of the Holy Spirit.

If you are prone to self-pity or tend to be overly emotional, you will need to pray for strength to keep yourself from needless exacerbations of sad memories. There were times in my fleeting hopelessness about the future when I wanted to wallow in my grief. It wasn't wise, it didn't honor God, and it fostered despair. To counter it, I confessed my sin to God and asked for his forgiveness. I came to the realization that I was focused on myself rather than on him. It also helped me to call a friend or involve myself in physical exercise.

Listening to popular music from the time in which my husband and I fell in love and deepened our relationship was excruciating after his death. Take care how much of this you expose yourself to. Do not needlessly increase your feelings of sadness, even though it can trigger memories you don't want to lose.

Be alert to particular times of the day, week, month, or year in which feelings of sadness may be intensified. I was caught by surprise when the seasons changed. Since my husband died in the late fall and the winter seemed to worsen my sadness, I was looking forward to the coming of spring. But when it arrived, I felt sad in a different way. The change of seasons, rather than being refreshing, reminded me that my husband would not be with me to enjoy the things we liked to do together in the spring such as working in the yard and going on long walks. With the coming of each season that first year and the next, I grieved the loss of his presence in the things we would not be doing together.

A PSALM FOR TIMES OF DISTRESS

Shortly after my husband died I read and meditated on Psalm 31 for several weeks. Parts of this poem expressed how I was feeling. Let's look at some selected verses from this psalm. Below each verse I've inserted how the verse spoke to my experience of grief:

> In you, O LORD, do I take refuge;
> > let me never be put to shame;
> > in your righteousness deliver me! (v. 1)

THE UNDISTRACTED WIDOW

Lord, I feel scared and lonely, but I know that you can deliver me from my fears. You hide me in the shadow of your wings. You want me to seek refuge in you from my painful emotions. I am afraid of dishonoring you. Please keep me from the shame of wrongly representing your involvement in my life at this time. And deliver me from my flesh. It is weak and liable to tempt me to cast aspersions on your love for me.

> I will rejoice and be glad in your steadfast love,
>> because you have seen my affliction;
>> you have known the distress of my soul. (v. 7)

You see how I am suffering the loss of my husband. You know how distressed I am in my heart and soul. I feel totally empty inside. Sometimes it's hard to breathe or I forget to breathe. But when I remember that you see me, and I remind myself that you care for me, I begin to rejoice—faintly at first but enough to be glad in your never-ending love for me.

> Be merciful to me, O LORD, for I am in distress;
>> my eyes grow weak with sorrow,
>> my soul and my body with grief.
> My life is consumed by anguish
>> and my years by groaning;
>> my strength fails because of my affliction,
>> and my bones grow weak. (vv. 9–10 NIV)

My vision is blurry from floods of tears. The eye of my soul has trouble focusing on you because grief keeps intruding and obscuring my sight. Both my body and my soul are exhausted from mourning. I am so sad. I feel like the world is going on without me. O Lord, I am in desperate need of your grace to lift me above my distress.

> But I trust in you, O LORD;
>> I say, "You are my God." (v. 14)

Because you are my God, because you are willing to call me your own, because I know you have been trustworthy in all of my life, I trust you now. *You have not changed. You are still the God on whom I will lean for all that I need. It feels like my entire world has changed, but you remain the same—my faithful friend, my Lord, my God! I am starting to feel hopeful.*

> I had said in my alarm,
>> "I am cut off from your sight."
> But you heard the voice of my pleas for mercy
>> when I cried to you for help. (v. 22)

When I feel so alone, it feels like you are not here with me. This alarms me and I cry out to you like a little child in a dark room: "Father, help me!" And I find that you are still with me; you have not left me—you promised that you never would. And you keep your promises.

> Be strong, and let your heart take courage,
>> all you who wait for the LORD! (v. 24)

By your grace, I will wait and take courage that you are at work even in this time of sorrow. In my weakness I will be strong because I can do all things through Christ who strengthens me. He constantly infuses into my soul his love and his grace through his Spirit. You, Lord, are my tender shepherd; I have everything I need. I am at peace in your love. I have hope in my heart because of who you are.

God's Word speaks clearly and unfalteringly into our grief. We do not need to look elsewhere for guidance, help, and hope as we grieve.

BE ENCOURAGED, BE HOPEFUL

We may lament to God about our grief and loss but not in an accusatory way. The prophet Habakkuk lamented to God when God used a sinful nation to chasten Israel, but in the end Habakkuk prayed:

> Though the fig tree should not blossom,
>> nor fruit be on the vines,

the produce of the olive fail
> and the fields yield no food,
the flock be cut off from the fold
> and there be no herd in the stalls,
yet I will rejoice in the LORD;
> I will take joy in the God of my salvation.
GOD, the Lord, is my strength;
> he makes my feet like the deer's;
> he makes me tread on my high places. (Hab. 3:17–19)

Habakkuk was confident in the faithfulness, love, and justice of God. Even when he was trembling from hearing the advancing enemy army, Habakkuk rejoiced in God. We must do the same. Even when our hearts are breaking from the heaviness of grief, we can choose to rejoice in who God is and in what he will do on our behalf. It is evident in the Scriptures that God understands our sorrow, especially when we look at the sufferings of Christ. Because Christ was willing to suffer and die on behalf of his people, our sorrows are temporary rather than permanent. They are limited to life in this world.

We grieve the loss of those we love, but we do not grieve as those who have no hope of heaven and no hope of seeing again those who die in Christ.

> But we do not want you to be uninformed, brothers, about those who are asleep, that you may not grieve as others do who have no hope. For since we believe that Jesus died and rose again, even so, through Jesus, God will bring with him those who have fallen asleep. For this we declare to you by a word from the Lord, that we who are alive, who are left until the coming of the Lord, will not precede those who have fallen asleep. For the Lord himself will descend from heaven with a cry of command, with the voice of an archangel, and with the sound of the trumpet of God. And the dead in Christ will rise first. Then we who are alive, who are left, will be caught up together with them in the clouds to meet the Lord in the air, and so we will always be with the Lord. *Therefore encourage one another with these words.* (1 Thess. 4:13–18)

"Asleep" in verse 13 is a euphemism for "dead." Paul wants the Thessalonian believers to know that those who have died in Christ are with him in heaven. In his commentary on 1 Thessalonians, Leon Morris says:

> Death has been overcome by the risen Lord, and that has transformed the whole situation for those who are in him. . . .
>
> Paul is not saying that Christians never grieve, they have their sorrows like other people (cf. Phil. 2:27). But they sorrow as those who have an abiding hope. The apostle is not contrasting a lesser grief with a greater one; he is contrasting those with hope and those without it. When the non-Christian world is characterized as lacking hope it is probably not the absence of the hope of an afterlife that is primarily in mind, but the absence of the knowledge of God, much like those whom Paul describes as "without hope and without God in the world" (Eph. 2:12).[2]

The way you grieve will reveal much about what you believe about God.

GOD'S INVOLVEMENT

Because God is sovereign over all things, he is in control of your situation and mine. But God is not responsible for the presence of death in the world. Man, not God, is the initiator and sustainer of sin in the human race and thus death. We will all die because we all sin. But the good news for Christians is that we will *not* die a second death leading to eternal damnation:

> Just as it is appointed for man to die once, and after that comes judgment, so Christ, having been offered once to bear the sins of many, will appear a second time, not to deal with sin but to save those who are eagerly waiting for him. (Heb. 9:27–28)

Therefore, you can have hope that you will be reunited with your Christian husband when God calls you home to heaven.

Suppose you are uncertain as to whether your husband was a Christian. Only God knows with *absolute certainty* who is in heaven and who is not. Yet, we can have confidence that those who have persevered in the faith have gone to heaven. If you do not have that certainty regarding your spouse, you can pray and confidently leave it with God. Ask God to give you grace to entrust your concern to him and to leave it with him. He is sovereign and good and a just judge. Do not torture your mind about it. None whom God elects are lost, so you can let God's perfect integrity console your heart. Don't get trapped in excessive sorrow. Cultivate your love for Christ and anticipate with joy the day you will be with him in heaven. Our greatest hope lies in seeing Christ face-to-face.

Commenting on Job 14:1, "Man who is born of a woman is few of days and full of trouble," Charles Spurgeon says:

> We should love, but we should love with the love that expects death, and which expects separations. Our dear relations are but loaned to us, and the hour when we must return them to the lender's hand may be even at the door. . . .
>
> There is no single point in which we can hope to escape from the sharp arrows of affliction; out of our few days no one is safe from sorrow. . . .
>
> Beloved reader, don't set your affections upon things of earth; but seek those things which are above, for *here* the moth devours, and the thief breaks through, but *there* all joys are perpetual and eternal. The path of trouble is the way home.[3]

God has the right to give or to take life as he pleases because he is the sovereign Creator. Therefore, we must not rail against him in our sorrow. We must not accuse him of wrongdoing. Even in the deepest recesses of our souls we must purge out any ill will toward him regarding the death of our husband. Our Father wants us to come to him and express our true feelings, but this must be done in a respectful way and with confidence in his goodness.

THE WATCHING WORLD

A Christian widow's loss of her husband is not only about her suffering. It is an opportunity to manifest the power of God to comfort his people even in significant adversity. Martyn Lloyd-Jones pointed out:

> The world today is presenting us with a unique opportunity of telling men and women about "the unsearchable riches of Christ." We are being

watched, we are being observed; and many in their spiritual bankruptcy are wondering whether, after all, the answer is Christ. The world judges Him by what it sees in us. If we give the impression that, after all, to be a Christian does not help very much when there is a crisis, they will not listen to our message or look to Him. But if they find that we are entirely different from them, and able to maintain a calm and balance and peace and poise, and even joy in the midst of the hurricane of life, under God that may be the means of opening their eyes, and leading them to repentance, and bringing them to the Lord Jesus Christ and His "unsearchable riches."[4]

It may sound like a tall order to display God in this way, especially when you feel like you haven't an ounce of strength. God can give you that strength. You will delight his heart as you honor him. "Blessed is the man who remains steadfast under trial, for when he has stood the test he will receive the crown of life, which God has promised to those who love him" (James 1:12).

> Jesus! What a help in sorrow!
> While the billows o'er me roll;
> Even when my heart is breaking,
> He, my Comfort, helps my soul.
> Hallelujah! What a Savior!
> Hallelujah! What a Friend!
> Saving, helping, keeping, loving,
> He is with me to the end.[5]

MANAGING YOUR EMOTIONS

Set your minds on things that are above, not on things that are on earth.
For you have died, and your life is hidden with Christ in God.
When Christ who is your life appears,
then you also will appear with him in glory.

COLOSSIANS 3:2–4

In her novel *Sense and Sensibility*, Jane Austen presents the story of two sisters with decidedly different temperaments. The eldest daughter, Elinor, has such a firm grip on her emotions that it is an irritant to her sister Marianne, who believes in wearing her heart on her sleeve. As the story unfolds, we witness the consequences to both sisters of their different approaches to life. Elinor is all sense and Marianne is all sensibility until the events of their lives lead them to appreciate the strengths of the other. In this chapter, we will apply the sense of Scripture while also rejoicing in the sensibility of a biblically guided and rich emotional life.

RIGHT THINKING PRODUCES RIGHT FEELINGS

We are not robots. God created us with the ability to respond emotionally to him and to the people and circumstances in our lives. The fact that we are emotional creatures is a good thing. The problem comes in when we do not manage our emotions so that God is glorified and our lives are enriched. Our emotions give us clues to how we think and what we believe about our situation, our God, and ourselves.

It is very important when grieving the loss of our husband not to put our trust in how we feel and not to function according to our emotions. Consider this wise counsel from Jerry Bridges:

> If we are to trust God in adversity, we must use our minds in those times to reason through the great truths of God's sovereignty, wisdom, and love as they are revealed to us in the Scriptures. We must not allow our emotions to hold sway over our minds. Rather, we must seek to let the truth of God rule our minds. Our emotions must become subservient to the truth. This does not mean we do not feel the pain of adversity and heartache. We feel it keenly. Nor does it mean we should seek to bury our emotional pain in a stoic-like attitude. We are meant to feel the pain of adversity, but we must resist allowing that pain to cause us to lapse into hard thoughts about God.[1]

The great truths of Scripture help us to know God better and will provide a rock on which to base our thinking. When our beliefs about God are consistent with his Word then our feelings will arise and flow from those truths. As we reason out the truths about our situation, our emotional responses will be appropriate to the reality of what God is doing in our lives. This is the way to be stable emotionally.

Patti McCarthy Broderick lost her husband suddenly when he died in a military plane crash. Early in her widowhood, she approached God in this way:

> I was not coming to the Creator and Sustainer of this universe respectfully, humbly to ask questions about the situation He has ordained for me and ways He would use me. I was coming to rant and rave at an unfair God who did not know what He was doing or could not be trusted to do what is best in my life and in the lives of those I care about.
>
> Whining to God removed the certainty of God's character and His wisdom from my focus and replaced them with my desires. The result of my whining was that it shook my whole world and stripped me of God's perfect peace and joy. There is comfort and security in the knowledge that, even in the most frightening and confusing times of our lives, that the character and truth of God remain intact.[2]

Many widows feel this same way—devastated, despairing, and complaining toward God. Patti recognized the error in her thinking and in her approach to God. She writes:

I knew I would have to learn how to relish the joy of God's presence in my life and to count on His presence alone as I dreamed of the future. . . . A mind focused on what is lost is much more likely to experience discouragement and hopelessness than one focused on the joys ahead God is able to provide.[3]

Though reeling initially from the shock of her husband's death, she gained control over her emotions by depending on God to think rightly about her circumstances.

TWO SEPARATE WORLDS

Some widows talk to their deceased husbands or write letters to them. Though primarily a method to allow a widow to release her emotions or to comfort her, I do not recommend either of these practices. It is tempting to want to talk to our husband even though he is dead. We want to be able to tell him about our day or about life's events. If we visit his gravesite, we want to say something to him—"Oh, how I miss you! Oh, how hard life is without you!" Why would anyone object to this seemingly innocent practice?

I cannot find endorsement in the Scriptures for talking to the dead. Rather, I find what looks like evidence to the contrary.[4] "But," objected a widow with whom I was chatting at a conference, "my husband is not dead, he is alive in heaven, and I talk to him there." But the Scriptures do not endorse this practice even if we think of the deceased as still alive and living in heaven. If our husband was a Christian, he is alive in heaven, but he is dead to this world.[5]

Nevertheless, what is the harm of engaging in sentimental fantasy where a widow "talks" to her husband? My objection is that besides denying reality, it inhibits the ongoing growth of a warm, vibrant, and precious relationship with the Lord. It hampers the continued development of intimate conversation with God through his Spirit. Christ will abundantly comfort us. We must not demand that this comfort come in the form that we desire. Ask him to give you grace to accept the way in which he chooses to comfort and communicate with you.

The Holy Spirit is alive and present with and in his people. It is far better to be in the Word and in prayer asking God to be your source of living love and comfort than to be engaged in a specious therapeutic technique that will not produce real effects. "Talking to the deceased . . . shortcuts Scripture's insistence and gracious offer for us to find every needed grace in the provision of Christ. It trades truth for fiction, and no Christian should be content with that."[6]

Fill your mind with thoughts of the Lord, and soon your emotions will attach themselves to him in ever-increasing devotion and adoration. What we love, whom we love, preoccupies our thinking. What we think about all day captures our hearts. Martyn Lloyd-Jones writes:

> The things we are to think about must be compatible with the gospel. As Christian people we must see to it that the whole of our life, our very thoughts and ideas, everything, are under the mighty control of the risen Lord. Every thought must be brought into subjection to him. As we read in 2 Corinthians 10:5, we must bring everything into captivity to Christ; Christ must control our minds and the whole of our thinking.[7]

Trust the Lord to bring you the comfort you need in your sorrow. Walk with him step by step through your day and let your mind be set on him in loving friendship.

TOWARD AN ORDERLY MIND

It is possible to control our thoughts. The Scriptures tell us what we should be thinking about:

> If then you have been raised with Christ, seek the things that are above, where Christ is, seated at the right hand of God. Set your minds on things that are above, not on things that are on earth. For you have died, and your life is hidden with Christ in God. (Col. 3:1–3)
> You keep him in perfect peace whose mind is stayed on you, because he trusts in you. (Isa. 26:3)

Though it may be much harder to control our thoughts when we are under extreme duress, it is still possible and well worth the effort. Here are some ways to bring order to what may seem like chaos in your mind:

- pray and ask God to help you direct your thoughts for his honor and your good;
- identify what you are feeling;
- label that feeling correctly;[8]
- explore your thoughts to see how they engendered those feelings;
- identify what beliefs you hold that led to those thoughts;
- compare those beliefs to the truths of Scripture;
- rid yourself of wrong beliefs through confession, repentance, and accepting biblical truth;
- coach yourself to think on the things that are true according to the Bible;
- monitor what feelings follow your new beliefs and thoughts.

Take notice of what you are thinking. What scenarios are playing out in your mind? Ask yourself questions. "What is bothering me?" "What is on my mind?" Martyn Lloyd-Jones writes that we ought to coach ourselves, talk to ourselves, and reason with ourselves.[9] We aren't to simply drift along through a day letting our feelings lead our thoughts wherever they want to go. You may find keeping a chart of your feelings and thoughts helpful in identifying their source. Ask God to enable you to exercise self-discipline through the power of his Spirit so that you can think in godly ways. Ask the Spirit to guide your mind by way of the description in Philippians 4:8:

> Finally, brothers, whatever is true, whatever is honorable, whatever is just, whatever is pure, whatever is lovely, whatever is commendable, if there is any excellence, if there is anything worthy of praise, think about these things.

That verse is not so much a laundry list of separate kinds of things to think about as a description of the way to have peace in your mind. The context both before and after verse 8 is that of gaining the peace of God. And the most powerful of these thoughts will be those set on the gospel of Jesus Christ.[10]

DEPRESSION

Shock, confusion, and depressed feelings are common among the newly bereaved. Whether your husband died suddenly or slowly, your emo-

tions have probably been like a sickening roller-coaster ride. We grieving spouses must not confuse intense sadness with depression. Feelings
of deep sadness over the death of a husband are completely normal and
highly appropriate. Unless we have been diagnosed with a physical condition that warrants medication, my suggestion is that we address this
deep sadness with biblical counsel rather than reaching for medicine.
Psychotropic medications often have annoying and persistent side effects.
If you think you need them, try to limit them to short-term use. Find a
trusted friend who will listen with empathy. Many studies have shown the
efficacy of friendship counseling. And don't neglect to pour out your heart
to your Best Friend!

We also do well to exercise discernment in joining a bereavement
group. The secular groups are devoid of biblical principles and comfort.
But even the groups that purport to be Christian are sometimes lacking
in sound biblical teaching. If you are offered the opportunity to watch a
Christian video series on grief, be discerning. Often these series are a mix-
ture of man-centered ideas with some Bible verses sprinkled throughout.
Be sure to read the Scriptures and books by trusted Christian authors like
those mentioned in the suggested reading list at the end of this book.

In my lowest moments, the Lord always provided abundant help.
When the psalmist was in a deeply downcast condition, he asked himself
this question:

> Why are you cast down, O my soul,
>   and why are you in turmoil within me?
> Hope in God; for I shall again praise him,
>   my salvation and my God. (Ps. 42:11)

Notice that he answered his own questions by coaching himself to hope in
God. The apostle Paul counseled the Corinthians with these words:

> No temptation has overtaken you that is not common to man. God is
> faithful, and he will not let you be tempted beyond your ability, but with
> the temptation he will also provide the way of escape, that you may be
> able to endure it. (1 Cor. 10:13)

God will enable you to endure the trial of losing your husband as you lean on him and trust him. Your heavenly Father is watching over you with love.

SELF-PITY

John Younts provides us with these very insightful words about our attitude toward God's control over our lives:

> Anyone who thinks he deserves to have life unfold as he pleases is bound to be frustrated and discontent much of the time. People who don't get their own way in life begin to feel resentful and sorry for themselves. Self-pity is a powerful, negative attitude that gives rise to many, many excuses for sin. People fall into Satan's trap of giving themselves "permission" to sin to compensate for the difficulties and trials they've had to bear. Self-pity is a direct rejection of God's control. It is saying, "I don't like what you've done in my life, and I absolutely will not be content. I can't change it, so I'll just be angry and miserable."[11]

Self-pity easily leads to bitterness over time. A more sorry state is hard to imagine.

LETHARGY

Exhaustion is common during early bereavement and can be a source of lethargic feelings. Another of the sources of lethargy is viewing excessive amounts of television. People who watch a lot of television tend to be more depressed than those who watch less. Watching TV is a significant temptation if you find yourself suddenly living alone. You can lift this dark curtain of lethargy by fixing your thoughts on the Lord through prayer, reading the Word, and finding ways to serve others. Physical exercise is another way to effectively address lethargy. Choose something you like to do and stick with it. Both your body and your mind will benefit from the mood-elevating effect of physical exercise.

A widow does not need to be the helpless victim of her emotions. When we are weak, God pours out his grace upon us. Ask him for power to get control over your emotions by directing your thoughts onto him and his kingdom. You are precious to him. Your well-being is his personal concern. All things are possible with God, even the ability to remain emotionally stable in the midst of tragedy.

> May the mind of Christ my Savior
> live in me from day to day
> By His love and power controlling
> all I do and say.

> May the Word of God dwell richly
> in my heart from hour to hour,
> So that all may see I triumph
> only through His power.[12]

11

OVERCOMING LONELINESS

She who is truly a widow, left all alone, has set her hope on God and
continues in supplications and prayers night and day.

1 TIMOTHY 5:5

Some years ago, the folk duo of Simon and Garfunkel had a best-selling song called "The Sound of Silence." One of the lines in the song says, "Silence like a cancer grows." Quietly, relentlessly, invasively, powerfully, silence can overcome the lonely grieving person. Silence and its cousin, stillness, intensify loneliness. But loneliness is not the exclusive province of the widow. Loneliness does not just happen when we are alone. People can feel lonely in a crowd. Married people can feel lonely. Children get lonely. Soldiers become lonely far from home on military duty.

THE CURE

Although not only the widowed are lonely, the loneliness of widows exhibits aspects that are particular to the loss of one's life partner. When two have been one, separating them brings pain. Nothing I had ever experienced in the past was like it. The loneliness of bereavement grabs hold of the widow and threatens to shake her faith. The one and only sure cure for loneliness lies in relationship with the Lord Jesus Christ. He endured an unparalleled depth of loneliness on the cross. Jesus cried out as his Father turned his face away from him. He felt the full weight of being forsaken. While Jesus was bearing the sins of his people, God the Father could not look on him. Though Christ himself was sinless, he bore our sin and the punishment it required. And so the eternal fellowship and companionship of Father and Son were broken temporarily as Christ paid the penalty for sin.

Before the crucifixion, Jesus had never known a time when he was not in perfect and rich relationship with his Father. That is why the Lord can empathize with your feelings of loneliness. No matter how deep and devastating they may be, the consolation of Christ is deeper still. We have a great High Priest who is able to sympathize with our weaknesses, who in every respect has been tempted as we are, yet he did not sin. Therefore, let's with full confidence draw near to the throne of grace that we may receive mercy and find grace to help in time of need (Heb. 4:14–16).

In Psalm 62 we find an expression of David's serene and confident hope in God despite being in very difficult circumstances:

> For God alone my soul waits in silence;
>   from him comes my salvation.
> He only is my rock and my salvation,
>   my fortress; I shall not be greatly shaken. . . .
> For God alone, O my soul, wait in silence,
>   for my hope is from him.
> He only is my rock and my salvation,
>   my fortress; I shall not be shaken.
> On God rests my salvation and my glory;
>   my mighty rock, my refuge is God.
> Trust in him at all times, O people;
>   pour out your heart before him;
>   God is a refuge for us. (vv. 1–2, 5–8)

Verse 1 says that "my soul waits in silence." Here is a good kind of silence; the silence of waiting upon God, of knowing that he is present with you. Verse 5 connects silence and waiting with hope. The stillness and silence of loneliness is a pathway to God. In your loneliness, go to him and seek his companionship through his Spirit. You will find that loneliness retreats and is not able to disturb your peace as it previously had.

THE SERENITY OF SOLITUDE

Jesus sought out solitude so that he could be with his Father and talk to him. After John the Baptist had been beheaded by orders from Herod, the Bible tells us, "Now when Jesus heard this, he withdrew from there in a boat to a desolate place by himself" (Matt. 14:13). After Jesus cleansed a leper of his dreaded disease, Luke writes, "But now even more the report about him went abroad, and great crowds gathered to hear him and to be healed of their infirmities. But he would withdraw to desolate places and pray" (Luke 5:15–16).

During his earthly ministry Jesus spent much time alone with God the Father in prayer. We also need to seek God in prayer. "She who is truly a widow, left all alone, has set her hope on God and continues in supplications and prayers night and day" (1 Tim. 5:5). Prayer is essential to addressing loneliness. As we talk to our Father about our suffering, he will provide the grace we need to find in Christ our all in all. When loneliness begins to overtake us, we can stop what we are doing and go to our Father in humble, believing prayer and ask for grace to know him better.

Let's look at part of Psalm 102—a psalm that Derek Kidner describes as "a prayer which others who are near the end of their endurance can echo."[1] The words italicized after each stanza suggest a way to respond to the psalm so that your heart will be comforted by your heavenly Father:

> Hear my prayer, O LORD;
>> let my cry come to you! (v. 1)

Lord, when I feel so lonely, it seems like you are far, far, away.

> Do not hide your face from me
>> in the day of my distress!
> Incline your ear to me;
>> answer me speedily in the day when I call! (v. 2)

I am weighed down by this loneliness. I feel as though you do not see or hear me. My thoughts are scattered, and I need quick relief from my troubled feelings.

> My heart is struck down like grass and has withered;
>> I forget to eat my bread. (v. 4)

My spirit is weak and I've lost my appetite. A surge of loneliness has knocked me over. Battling against these lonely feelings has distracted me from thoughts of you. Lord, help me. Give me an undivided heart of devotion.

> I am like a desert owl of the wilderness,
>> like an owl of the waste places;
> I lie awake;
>> I am like a lonely sparrow on the housetop. (vv. 6–7)

I can't sleep because my mind keeps trying to figure out a way to face tomorrow. How can I endure another day in which the most vivid thing to me is my husband's absence? A lonely sparrow on a housetop—yes, I identify with that—so small, so alone. Lord, I ask that you would give me grace to know you as my greatest reality—that you would be more real to me than my loneliness.

> But you, O LORD, are enthroned forever;
>> you are remembered throughout all generations. (v. 12)

Thank you for every place in the Scriptures, Lord, where the word "but" changes the entire outlook for the better. Despite the suffering of loneliness, I will choose to praise you, to look for you, to remember you, to be glad in you, and to rejoice in you always because you are my God and you comfort me in my distress. I can breathe again; I can rest securely in your love. I know I can go on and that you will guide me and continue your love to me.

The remedy that God has provided for those who are lonely is himself. Loneliness is meant to teach us to turn toward the Lord.

SPECIFIC STRATEGIES

If living alone is contributing to your loneliness, you might want to consider some ways to impact that situation. I lived alone for several years after my husband's death until I saw an opportunity to help a friend who has been preparing to go to the mission field in Europe. I offered to share my home with her, and doing so has been a blessing for me in many ways. You, too, might want to consider opening your home to missionaries on furlough or to those engaged in "pre-field" ministry, or you might think of other ways to share you home.

If holiday time is especially stressful because of loneliness, write down some ways you can bring about a solution. It is helpful to recognize that our holiday celebrations won't be the way they formerly were. We may feel the need to grieve the loss of the old traditions, but then it is time to move on and accept the fact that life is different now. We must make new plans and be flexible. It is best not to expect others to reach out to include us. They may, and it will be nice if they do, but if that does not happen, we must do the reaching out. Be sure to investigate the possibilities well before the holiday arrives. Find new ways to serve others. Or seize the occasion to do some traveling.

We can volunteer our time to help in our local church, in neighborhoods, and communities. I know a widow who volunteers in a local elementary school. Or we can *be* the student and take a class, learning a language, or to paint, or to gain any new skill. Sitting around and letting tidal waves of loneliness overcome you is not wise. Think of ways to get out of the house and serve to the best of your ability. When we serve God and others, we are more likely to forget ourselves.

CYBER-SEARCHING FOR COMPANIONSHIP

In order to mitigate lonely feelings, we widows sometimes pursue solutions that require caution. I'm thinking in particular of online matchmaking. Whether Christians should utilize online matchmaking services is a controversial subject; obviously, the Bible does not speak specifically to this issue. But, as in all other questions about life and practice, we can certainly find guidance in the Scriptures about it.

Nancy Leigh DeMoss gives a well-thought-out response to a question posed by a woman listening to her radio broadcast, *Revive Our Hearts*. The listener wanted to know what Nancy's views are regarding Christian matchmaking Web sites, and I've summarized them:

- It is important to make a choice, based on the teachings of Scripture, not to pursue marriage or men. By God's design, marriage is to be an earthly picture of a heavenly reality. Christ came from heaven as the bridegroom, and the church is his bride. He pursues; the church responds. In marriage, the man pursues and the woman responds. For a Christian woman to utilize an Internet matchmaking service puts her in the position of the pursuer.
- Accept your singleness as a gift from God and do not demand that he give you a husband. *Focus* on *being* the right person, not on *finding* the right person. If you are the woman God wants you to be and if he wants you to be married, he will bring a spouse to you. If God doesn't have a husband for you, you don't want the alternative.
- Making use of matchmaking Web sites might be an expression of a lack of faith. It seems to exhibit an unwillingness to wait for God, of fixing what is regarded as delayed timing on God's part.
- The best choice is to pursue intimacy with God, seeking earnestly to know him, and allowing God to fulfill your deepest needs. Trust, wait, rest. God is faithful and will fulfill his purposes in your life.[2]

Too hard, you're thinking? Unrealistic, you say? Old-fashioned, you believe? I encourage you to search the Scriptures thoroughly to test this approach.

Lydia Brownback recognizes the difficulties and dangers inherent in searching for a date or mate via an Internet matchmaking Web site. On her blog called "The Purple Cellar," she lists "seven drawbacks to think about when considering an attempt at cyber love."[3] Here are five of them:

1) *Lack of accountability.* Conducting a romantic relationship in a public setting while surrounded by trusted, godly people carries with it a built-in measure of protection that electronic romance just can't provide.
2) *Lack of exposure.* Regardless of the various screening techniques offered on relationship Web sites, you can't really know who you're dealing with. Personality profiles and compatibility scores just don't cut it. People can present themselves any way they choose on screen.

3) *Possible lack of trust in God.* If God hasn't brought a suitable mate into the picture, doesn't it stand to reason that perhaps it just isn't his time to do so?

4) *Stewardship of resources.* Are the dollars and hours spent at the computer the most fruitful thing we can do for God's kingdom?

5) *The suspicion factor.* If a man is leading an active, full life and is involved in his church, then why is he looking elsewhere to meet someone?

You are likely aware that over half the people who utilize these online dating sites lie when filling out their personal profile data. Paying to access information that is not reliable over half the time seems unwise.

A somewhat new phenomenon is whole Web sites dedicated to exposing those who lie, stalk, masquerade as single when married, and commit other unseemly behaviors on matchmaking Web sites. You may object that you know people who have married someone they met online and the relationships worked out fine. But others know people who met online and the resulting relationships are dreadful.

Perhaps, at this point, you are thinking to yourself that the ordinary means of meeting people has its own pitfalls, and with that I agree. My personal experience in dating since becoming a widow has had its share of undulating aspects. I have not actively sought to date, but opportunities have come to me through the usual means of friends and acquaintances— traditional matchmaking.

BACK TO THE FUTURE

Not having dated since my college days, the thought of going out as part of a couple with anyone other than my husband seems weird to me. I asked myself a lot of questions beforehand. Some of the questions were substantive: Why am I doing this? Is this what God wants me to do, or am I just going with the flow? Do I have expectations of what will come of this? Other questions were frivolous: Just how much effort do I need to put into this? (I hope not much!) Do I need a new hairstyle? Is my makeup right? Are these clothes okay? Am I too skinny or too fat? Too short or too tall? (No, forget that one; everyone is taller than I am). Too intelligent or too dull? Too serious or too silly? Too young or too old? Back and forth went the questions in my mind. I felt like I was back in my teens. Ugh! So I counseled myself to throw out all the frivolous questions and concentrate on the substantive ones, and with trepidation, I proceeded to engage in this back-to-the-future enterprise.

Even if someone comes recommended to you, even if the man goes to your church, even if he is in a position of leadership at a church, it is a good idea not to make assumptions based on those circumstances. Exercise caution and be careful what you disclose about yourself. If you correspond by e-mail, remember that you never know where an e-mail message will end up. Ask yourself before you hit the "send" button how you will feel if your message is forwarded without your prior knowledge and permission.

In the same article by Nancy Leigh DeMoss that I mentioned earlier, she tells of a woman who wrote to her about how alone she had felt over the last ten years. The woman said, "Sometimes the desperation to find a husband outweighs my common sense." But she learned from her mistakes and came to see how important it is to maintain high standards of behavior. You and I want to conduct ourselves in a manner worthy of our calling in Christ. I am so thankful that God enabled me to conduct myself in honorable ways, to never write an e-mail message that I would be ashamed for the whole world to see, and to end a relationship when it was clear that God was not at the center. I give my heavenly Father all the credit and bless him for being so good to me by protecting me and giving me the strength to do what was right. He has no favorites. He can and will do the same for you if you ask him.

Whether single or married, the goal of the life of a Christian must be the same: glorifying God and enjoying him. The loneliness of widowhood is intended by design to help you know God better—to know him in ways you have not known him before.

> When I am sad at heart, teach me thy way!
> When earthly joys depart, teach me thy way!
> In hours of loneliness, in times of dire distress,
> in failure or success, teach me thy way![4]

FACING YOUR FEARS

Do not fear, for I am with you; do not anxiously look about you,
for I am your God. I will strengthen you, surely I will help you,
surely I will uphold you with My righteous right hand.

ISAIAH 41:10 (NASB)

"One man's trash is another man's treasure." You've heard that saying. And it seems that one man's fear is another man's thrill.

TOP TEN LISTS

Using any computer search engine, type in the phrase "Top Ten Fears," and you will find a myriad of lists of fears held by people in general and also in specific occupations or life situations. Speaking in public paralyzes many people but some of us are energized by it. Flying in airplanes scares a number of people but others enjoy it. Spiders strike fear in some hearts, but then there are those who cozy up to tarantulas as pets. Fear of heights is common but bungee jumpers hop over bridge railings headfirst toward the water. I even found a list of the top ten fears of writers. It seemed good to ignore that list. In this case, ignorance is bliss.

What about those of us who are widowed? What are our fears? I don't worry about strapping on a bungee cord and hopping off the nearest bridge, but there are fears in being a widow that I struggle against. What are yours? The top fears of widows seem to fall into these categories:

- Fear of the future
- Fear of being isolated
- Fear of changing relational dynamics

- Fear of living alone
- Fear of running out of money
- Fear of getting sick and having no one to help

While we cannot exhaustively address all aspects of these fears in this chapter, we can explore overarching principles that will enable us to faithfully meet the challenges of each category.[1] First, however, we need to realize that not all fear is bad.

FEAR OF THE LORD

The Bible instructs us that there is one kind of fear that is good and wise. That fear is the fear of the Lord. What exactly does this mean? One of the best explanations I have read comes from Sinclair Ferguson, who is a pastor and seminary professor. In an article entitled, "The Fear of the Lord," Ferguson notes that we get confused about what it means to fear the Lord because we think of fear only as a negative emotion to be avoided. The fear of the Lord, however, is a good kind of fear. When we faithfully fear God, all our lesser fears leave us. Christians have been delivered from a terror-type fear of the Lord because God has poured out his grace on us and forgiven our sins in Christ. Ferguson points out four aspects of fear of the Lord in an effort to define what it is:

> True fear of God almost defies definition, because it is really a synonym for the heartfelt worship of God for who and what He is. It is at one and the same time (1) a consciousness of being in the presence of True Greatness and Majesty; (2) a thrilling sense of privilege; (3) an overflow of respect and admiration; and perhaps supremely, (4) a sense that His opinion about my life is the only thing that really matters.
>
> To someone who fears God, His fatherly approval means everything, and the loss of it is the greatest of all griefs. To fear God is to have a heart that is sensitive to both His God-ness and His graciousness.[2]

So, fearing the Lord involves regarding him with the greatest respect and reverence because we know the greatness of his being. We hallow his name.

We don't live terrified of God but, instead, we live delightedly awed by him and drawn to him in love and the deepest respect. This godly fear of him will lead us to get all other fears in perspective, enabling us to eliminate them or so minimize them as to see them eventually expire. "Charm is deceitful, and beauty is vain, but a woman who fears the LORD is to be praised" (Prov. 31:30). Now let's go back to our list and look at our fears in the light of the fear of the Lord.

FEAR OF THE FUTURE

Fear associated with the future dwells on things that are not real and may never be real. Worrying about what's going to happen to us in the future is completely useless, yet it is hard to shake. Fear of the future is a sin against the God who holds the future of each of us widows in his loving and faithful hands. Take your "What if . . . ?" questions to God and ask him to change them into words of praise for his promised provision of all you need.

When Jesus began his public ministry, he preached these words in the Sermon on the Mount: "Therefore do not be anxious about tomorrow, for tomorrow will be anxious for itself. Sufficient for the day is its own trouble" (Matt. 6:34). We need to walk by faith in God and trust him for each day that comes. It is fine to make reasonable plans for our future, but it is wrong to worry and fret over it. We are to live in the present, ready for the future, with one desire only—to glorify God. "Let not your heart envy sinners, but continue in the fear of the LORD all the day. Surely there is a future, and your hope will not be cut off" (Prov. 23:17–18). "The fear of the LORD is the beginning of wisdom; all those who practice it have a good understanding" (Ps. 111:10).

FEAR OF BEING ISOLATED

Next on our list is fear of being isolated and alone. Adjusting to being single again is a difficult struggle. Finding ways to fit in even at church is often very hard. Sometimes, weary from exercising much effort in this regard, it seems easier to give up and resign ourselves to the situation. However, since Christians are indwelt by the Spirit of Christ, we are never alone. "Have I not commanded you? Be strong and courageous. Do not be frightened, and do not be dismayed, for the LORD your God is with you wherever you go" (Josh. 1:9).

We are always in the presence of the Lord and can have rich communion with him (1 John 1:3). This fellowship occurs as we develop our friendship with him similar to the way we pursue friendship with our brothers and sisters in Christ. We spend time with the Lord in his Word, in prayer, and in service for him. In these times, we grow close to him and know him as a real, living companion.

> Rejoice in the Lord always; again I will say, rejoice! Let your gentle spirit be known to all men. *The Lord is near.* Be anxious for nothing, but in everything by prayer and supplication with thanksgiving let your requests be made known to God. And the peace of God, which surpasses all comprehension, will guard your hearts and your minds in Christ Jesus. (Phil. 4:4–7 NASB)

As we exercise courage, reach out to people, and serve others, our times of being alone will be reduced, which goes a long way toward banishing fears of being socially isolated. "The fear of the LORD is the beginning of wisdom, and the knowledge of the Holy One is insight" (Prov. 9:10).

FEAR OF CHANGING FAMILY DYNAMICS

Familial fear comes from a concern that the absence of our spouse will detrimentally affect relationships within our extended family. Surely the dynamics do change. Yet this does not need to be a negative factor, and it won't be unless we dwell on it and make it one. God is in this with us and wants us to be a testimony to his greatness and goodness as we minister love and grace to our family members. The dynamics will shift as they always do when someone is added to or subtracted from a group. But if we truly love and serve our family, this shift in dynamics can be a positive experience as we interact with our family and possess a joyful, loving spirit. "In the fear of the LORD one has strong confidence, and his children will have a refuge" (Prov. 14:26).

FEAR OF LIVING ALONE

Fear of living alone is one of the biggest concerns of many widows. Ultimately our physical safety rests in God's hands and that is where we must bring our fears about it. On this whole earth, no place is 100 percent safe. Life is full of risks and dangers from the moment of conception. There is a sense, however, in which Christians are entirely safe and even invincible and indestructible. If we are walking in obedience to God and depending on him to shelter us, we are safe. Nothing is going to happen to us without God's knowledge. He has determined the number of our days on this earth, and nothing can change that. I do not mean to suggest that bad things won't happen to us, but we can rest assured that whatever does happen is because of God's love and not because he is punishing us. In the first letter of Peter we find these words:

> For this is a gracious thing, when, mindful of God, one endures sorrows while suffering unjustly. For what credit is it if, when you sin and are beaten for it, you endure? But if when you do good and suffer for it you endure, this is a gracious thing in the sight of God. For to this you have been called, because Christ also suffered for you, leaving you an example, so that you might follow in his steps. (2:19–21)

If we are walking in obedience and we meet with adverse circumstances, we must believe that these things are happening for our good to make us more like Christ (see Romans 8).

FEAR OF RUNNING OUT OF MONEY

As I write this chapter, the world is in an economic crisis. Not one of us has escaped its effects. While this crisis has produced many hardships, not all its effects have been negative.[3] Many of us lost money we invested for the future, and the loss is causing us to take a hard look at exactly where our dependence lies. We may be seeing how weak our trust in God has been. We need to believe God's promise in Philippians 4:19: "My God will supply every need of yours according to his riches in glory in Christ Jesus." Speaking to the Israelites, God said:

> For every beast of the forest is mine,
>   the cattle on a thousand hills.

I know all the birds of the hills,
and all that moves in the field is mine.
If I were hungry, I would not tell you,
for the world and its fullness are mine.
Do I eat the flesh of bulls
or drink the blood of goats?
Offer to God a sacrifice of thanksgiving,
and perform your vows to the Most High,
and call upon me in the day of trouble;
I will deliver you, and you shall glorify me. (Ps. 50:10–15)

Your heavenly Father owns everything. You are his precious child. Whatever you truly need, he will never fail to provide for you. "Therefore do not be anxious, saying, 'What shall we eat?' or 'What shall we drink?' or 'What shall we wear?'" (Matt. 6:31). Money, clothes, shelter, and everything else you need are all within the power of almighty God to give you.

FEAR OF GETTING SICK AND HAVING NO ONE TO HELP

One of my fears after my husband died was getting sick and having no one to help me. Since then, I've been in the emergency room twice, hospitalized overnight once, and had to call 911 once for myself—all this because of adverse reactions to antibiotics. Life is like a theater play in which we are the actors and God is the director. He is behind the scenes directing everything. He is invisible and powerful. Our Father never leaves us, never abandons us, and always does what is best for us. "The fear of the LORD prolongs life, but the years of the wicked will be short" (Prov. 10:27).

FROM FEAR TO FAITH

The famous nineteenth-century preacher Charles Spurgeon exhorted Christians to wait patiently for the Lord and trust in him in the midst of their troubles:

> In seasons of severe trial, Christians have nothing on earth in which to
> trust, and we are therefore compelled to cast ourselves on our God alone.
> When we are burdened with troubles so pressing and so peculiar, that we

cannot tell them to anyone but our God, we may be thankful for them; for we will learn more of our Lord then than at any other time.

Now that you have only your God to trust, see that you put your full confidence in Him. Do not dishonor your Lord and Master by unworthy doubts and fears; but be strong in faith, giving glory to God. Show the world that your God is worth ten thousand worlds to you.

Show the strong how strong you are in your weakness when underneath you are the everlasting arms. Now is the time for feats of faith and valiant exploits. Be strong and very courageous, and the Lord your God shall certainly, as surely as He built the heavens and the earth, glorify Himself in your weakness, and magnify His might in the midst of your distress.[4]

God is your rock of refuge. Run to him with your cares and anxieties and cast them on him. His unwavering love will hold you up. "I sought the LORD, and he answered me and delivered me from all my fears" (Ps. 34:4). The Scriptures are full of comforting words regarding our fears.[5]

Psalm 23 is one that provides relief: "Even though I walk through the valley of the shadow of death, I will fear no evil, for you are with me; your rod and your staff, they comfort me" (v. 4). Notice the "I" and the "you" of the middle phrase. I will not fear *because* God is with me. The God who is your protector and defender (rod) and your director and guide (staff), who is omnipotent, can make you fearless. Have faith in him and walk fearlessly to his glory, "for God gave us a spirit not of fear but of power and love and self-control" (2 Tim. 1:7).

> Ye fearful saints, fresh courage take;
> the clouds ye so much dread
> are big with mercy, and shall break
> in blessings on your head.
>
> Judge not the Lord by feeble sense,
> but trust him for his grace;
> behind a frowning providence
> he hides a smiling face.[6]

BATTLING YOUR ADVERSARY

You are from God, little children, and have overcome them;
because greater is He who is in you than he who is in the world.
1 JOHN 4:4 (NASB)

In the September after my husband's death, I traveled to a nearby state to attend my niece's wedding. It was a beautiful day and a lovely location. Arriving home late that night, I crawled into bed tired from the trip and the emotional challenge of the first wedding I had attended as a widow. During the night, I was awakened several times by a scratching sound that seemed to be coming from near a window. Fatigue and disinterest kept me from getting up to find the source of the noise.

I awakened in the morning, made my way downstairs, fixed a cup of tea, and found my Bible. As I settled into a comfortable chair, I noticed out of the corner of my eye a small dark figure flying between the kitchen and the dining room. In the grogginess of my mind, I assumed it was a bird flying by the large windows. To my horror, a few moments later, that dark figure came flying directly at me. I ducked and dropped to the floor as I saw the hideous head and spread wings of a bat! Crawling across the room, I propped a door open and felt the bat graze the top of my head as it flew to its freedom. Heart racing, I rushed to the shower and used gobs of shampoo to wash that bat "right outta my hair."

The next weekend, I attended an all-day seminar at my church. While I was there, I left a trustworthy handyman at my house with a list of things that needed repairs. One of the items on the list was fixing a toilet on the second floor. The repair did not go well. Entering through the open garage door, I saw a gaping hole in the wall behind the second-floor bathroom. Inside the house there were holes in the powder room ceiling and the living room ceiling. Water was dripping down on the sofa and onto the wood floor. Hardly of the magnitude of Job's sufferings but still distressing.

Was it coincidence that on two successive weekends such upsetting circumstances occurred? Fate? Bad luck? No. I believe it was spiritual warfare meant to discourage me and tempt me to doubt God's love and care. By the grace of God, and only by his grace, I desire to live for God in a way that honors him. And I believe that Charles Spurgeon is right when he says that a bereaved widow who demonstrates faith in Christ manifests and magnifies God's grace.[1] Her adversaries will staunchly oppose such a mirror of God's love and goodness.

God's enemies are at work opposing the work of God in this world. It might be the last thing you'd expect in the midst of sorrow over the loss of your husband. After all, aren't things bad enough already? You miss him unspeakably, you're trying to handle all the matters that need to be dealt with after the death of a family member, and you're exhausted. Then you realize as time passes that a spiritual battle is going on in your life in a more pronounced and insidious way than usual.

THE BATTLE WITH THE WORLD

Ever since the day we became Christians, we have been battling against the world. Let's refresh our minds concerning the nature of this battle. We war against a worldly system that minimizes God and maximizes man. We don't want to get drawn in by the things that unbelievers crave. Instead, we want to live for God and for his kingdom. Writing to the Romans, the apostle Paul said, "Do not be conformed to this world, but be transformed by the renewal of your mind, that by testing you may discern what is the will of God, what is good and acceptable and perfect" (Rom. 12:2). We battle against the distractions that the world puts in front of our eyes as we seek first the kingdom of God. In the apostle John's first letter, we find this counsel:

> Do not love the world or the things in the world. If anyone loves the
> world, the love of the Father is not in him. For all that is in the world—

the desires of the flesh and the desires of the eyes and pride in possessions—is not from the Father but is from the world. (1 John 2:15–16)

I know Christian widows who have ended romantic relationships that
might have led to marriage because the men involved, though professing
to be Christians, did not have the same intensity of commitment to live
for God. Perhaps in the future God will bring someone into their lives and
bless them with another marriage, but until that time, these widows desire
to know the will of God for them and to avoid the things that worldly widows pursue, such as marriage for its own sake. They are willing to stand
alone and to resist the influences of the world system.

The worldly emphasis on outward appearance is something that all
Christian women need to resist and Christian widows are no exception.
Bereft of her husband, a widow might be tempted to spend inordinate time
and money on her appearance in an effort to feel better about herself or to
attract a man. Please don't misunderstand—it is fine to look nice and to
present ourselves in a pleasing way. But if we become preoccupied with
our appearance, we might be setting ourselves up as an idol and following
the ways of the world.

THE BATTLE WITH THE FLESH

The word *flesh* is used in a number of ways in Scripture and does not
always have a negative sense. But what does the Bible mean when it talks
about the flesh as an opposing force, as a sinful influence? In terms of battling the flesh, it is that sinful nature in all human beings through which
they rebel against the will of God. But by virtue of the indwelling Holy
Spirit, we are able not to sin. We are able to deny the sinful flesh what it
is demanding. This denial of the flesh is a war, one which will never be
fully won until we get to heaven. Writing as a Christian to Christians in
his letter to the Romans, the apostle Paul said:

> For I know that nothing good dwells in me, that is, in my flesh. For I
> have the desire to do what is right, but not the ability to carry it out. For
> I do not do the good I want, but the evil I do not want is what I keep on
> doing. . . . Wretched man that I am! Who will deliver me from this body

of death? Thanks be to God through Jesus Christ our Lord! So then, I myself serve the law of God with my mind, but with my flesh I serve the law of sin. (7:18–19, 24–25)

Paul's description of not wanting to do what he does paints a picture for us of the battle against the flesh. He goes on to talk about this war between the flesh and the Holy Spirit who indwells us:

> Those who are in the flesh cannot please God. You, however, are not in the flesh but in the Spirit, if in fact the Spirit of God dwells in you. Anyone who does not have the Spirit of Christ does not belong to him. . . . So then, brothers, we are debtors, not to the flesh, to live according to the flesh. For if you live according to the flesh you will die, but if by the Spirit you put to death the deeds of the body, you will live. (Rom. 8:8–13).

What struggles with the flesh might be more prevalent in widowhood? We might be prone to self-pity, indolence, anxiety, depression, hopelessness, or anger. But since the Holy Spirit in us can give us victory over our flesh, we are not helpless in the face of this struggle.

THE BATTLE WITH THE DEVIL AND OTHER SUPERNATURAL OPPONENTS

Our final category in battling our adversaries is that of the Devil, also called Satan, who is the leader of the fallen angels called demons. God cast these fallen angels out of heaven. They are spiritual beings who are corrupt and hostile to God. Of these demons, J. I. Packer notes:

> Their minds are permanently set to oppose God, goodness, truth, the kingdom of Christ, and the welfare of human beings, and they have real if limited power and freedom of movement, though in Calvin's pictur-esque phrase they drag their chains wherever they go and can never hope to overcome God.[2]

The Devil and demons war against Christians because they hate Christ. The apostle Peter exhorted the early Christians to be alert regarding their enemy:

Be sober-minded; be watchful. Your adversary the devil prowls around like a roaring lion, seeking someone to devour. Resist him, firm in your faith, knowing that the same kinds of suffering are being experienced by your brotherhood throughout the world. And after you have suffered a little while, the God of all grace, who has called you to his eternal glory in Christ, will himself restore, confirm, strengthen, and establish you. (1 Pet. 5:8–10)

As I read Spurgeon's devotional book *Morning and Evening*, I gained important insight into the nature of the struggle I was having with grief, particularly as the days faded into evenings. In one entry he writes:

How similar the fiends of hell are to wolves at dusk, for when the flock of Christ is in a cloudy and dark day, and their sun seems to be going down, they [evil beings] hasten to tear and to devour. They will seldom attack the Christian in the daylight of faith, but in the gloom of soul conflict, they fall upon him. O You who have laid down Your life for the sheep, preserve them from the fangs of the wolf.[3]

I took his words to mean that when a Christian is in the midst of circumstances that are weighing heavily upon him, the forces of evil will attack him more fiercely. When you are down, expect that you will encounter a more intense battle with evil. You do not need to fear it, but you do need to be prepared for it.

Once I realized that the struggle was also coming from outside me, I armed myself more effectively for the battle. In Ephesians 6 we are given insight and direction concerning spiritual warfare. Verse 16 uses the word *all* twice: in *all* circumstances you can extinguish *all* the flaming darts of the Evil One. This is huge encouragement in the midst of warfare. Anything that the Devil and his cohorts throw at you can be snuffed out by the power of the Holy Spirit. Though the forces of evil are supernatural and far greater than human power, they are no match for the omnipotence of God. William Cowper brilliantly described the role of prayer in spiritual warfare:

Restraining pray'r, we cease to fight;
Pray'r makes the Christian's armour bright;

And Satan trembles, when he sees
The weakest saint upon his knees.[4]

The Devil is a powerful foe, but he is not God's equal. He is a created being, a fallen angel. Along with the other fallen angels, he wreaks havoc on God's creation. The good news is that at the cross Christ triumphed over the Devil and all the powers of evil. The Devil is not omnipotent, omniscient, or omnipresent, and he is a defeated foe. We know from Scripture, especially chapter 1 of the book of Job, that the Devil is under the control of God's sovereignty. In ways that we do not fully understand, God uses the Devil and demons for his own glory and purposes.

The Scriptures instruct us to resist the Devil, and then he will flee: "Submit yourselves therefore to God. Resist the devil, and he will flee from you. Draw near to God, and he will draw near to you" (James 4:7–8). As we draw near to God in humble dependence on his protection, God gives us grace and strengthens our faith. If we remain anxious, it is a symptom of unbelief. Humble reliance on God produces a heart relieved of its fears.

In Christ's High Priestly Prayer, he prays for us in this way:

"I have given them your word, and the world has hated them because they are not of the world, just as I am not of the world. I do not ask that you take them out of the world, but that you keep them from the evil one" (John 17:14–15). When Christ died and rose from the dead, Satan was defeated. No basis for fear of the evil perpetrated by the Devil and demons exists for Christians. We are indwelt by the Spirit and Christ is at the right hand of the Father, and he has interceded for us that we would be kept safe from the powers of darkness. Speaking of the helpfulness of Christ, Arthur Pink makes the following observations:

> At such times [periods of bereavement] Satan is particularly active, launching his fiercest attacks, tempting them in various ways. Here is relief—real, present, all-sufficient relief. Turn your heart and eye to the Saviour and consider how well qualified He is to succor you. . . .
>
> He knows all about your case, fully understands your trials, and gauges the strength of your temptation. He is not an indifferent spectator, but full of compassion. . . .

Succor is a comprehensive word: it means "to befriend," "to assist those in need," "to strengthen the weak." But the Greek term is even more striking and beautifully expressive: it signifies to hasten in response to a cry of distress, literally to "run in to the call" of another. . . .

As angels ministered to Him after His conflict with Satan, so He ministers to us. Then no matter how dire your situation or acute your suffering, apply to Christ for relief and deliverance and count upon His help.[5]

Only God is powerful enough to keep us safe from evil supernatural beings. We do not speak to the Devil or demons; rather, we speak to God about them. Note that even good angels, who are powerful supernatural beings, defer to God to rebuke the Devil:

> When the archangel Michael, contending with the devil, was disputing about the body of Moses, he did not presume to pronounce a blasphemous judgment, but said, "The Lord rebuke you." (Jude 9)

Appeal to God for protection and resist the Devil through the Word and prayer and godly living. This is the way to be delivered from the powers of darkness.

FIGHT THE GOOD FIGHT

The sources of evil are not mere distractions. They are potentially powerful in keeping us from living for God. These sources of evil are our enemies. The world, the flesh, and the Devil all threaten to thwart our attempts at living undistracted, totally devoted, and unspeakably joyful lives for the Lord. To summarize our strategy for warfare, let's list the essentials:

- Keep alert
- Remember you are never alone or without divine resources
- Trust God and obey him
- Think and act biblically
- Recite Scripture to yourself
- Yield to the Holy Spirit's control
- Pray fervently and faithfully

- Be humble
- Persevere in resisting the Devil

We are in a battle because the Christian life is war. We know the outcome, and we will triumph over our enemies through Christ. Let's take seriously Paul's exhortation to Timothy and consider it our own: "Fight the good fight of the faith. Take hold of the eternal life to which you were called and about which you made the good confession in the presence of many witnesses" (1 Tim. 6:12).

> At the sign of triumph Satan's host doth flee;
> on then, Christian soldiers, on to victory:
> hell's foundations quiver at the shout of praise;
> brothers, lift your voices, loud your anthems raise.
> Onward, Christian soldiers, marching as to war,
> with the cross of Jesus going on before.[6]

14

LEARNING TO BE CONTENT IN YOUR CIRCUMSTANCES

Not that I am speaking of being in need,
for I have learned in whatever situation I am to be content.
PHILIPPIANS 4:11

Weather conditions upon takeoff from our local airport are often cloudy and overcast. Though it may look dreary from the ground, we are suddenly in glorious, sparkling sunshine when we reach cruising altitude. The air is clear and the light is brilliant. Right now in your life it may seem like you will never get off the ground into any sort of sunny place. It may be hard to believe there is a sun at all. You may be down under your circumstances, caught in the gloominess of grief. Just as we need the power of jet engines to fly above the clouds, we need the power of the Holy Spirit to consistently rise above our circumstances.

My five-year-old granddaughter Emma enjoys watching weather reports on television. She repeats some of the phrases she hears. One of her favorites is "Local Airport Delays." It sounds so funny to hear her sweet little voice parroting the announcement. But real delays and the waiting involved are always a trial. Widowhood is somewhat like being caught in an airport delay—one that seems to have no end. We want so badly to be out from under emotionally draining circumstances and into the sunshine of contentment. How can we reach cruising altitude when our situation seems to keep delaying our ascent?

How we pursue contentment and what the object of our contentment is reveals what or whom we worship. While human relationships can bring us comfort, *resting in and enjoying our union with Christ is the key*

119

to contentment. In John's Gospel we find these words of Jesus that teach us about our union with him:

> And I will ask the Father, and he will give you another Helper, to be with you forever, even the Spirit of truth, whom the world cannot receive, because it neither sees him nor knows him. You know him, for he dwells with you and will be *in* you. . . . In that day you will know that I am in my Father, and you *in* me, and I *in* you. (John 14:16–17, 20)
>
> I have said these things to you, that *in* me you may have peace. In the world you will have tribulation. But take heart; I have overcome the world. (John 16:33)

Instructing the early Christians about their union in Christ, the apostle Paul said: "But he who is joined to the Lord becomes one spirit with him" (1 Cor. 6:17). In this time of sorrow and loss, focus on your union with Christ. We are not bereft of his love. The love of Christ overflows to bring us contentment through our union in him. If our human relations are more near and dear to us than Christ, we will be awash in discontentment when they are separated from us.

TRUE BIBLICAL CONTENTMENT: WHAT IT IS

True biblical contentment is a grace given by God through his Spirit as he does his sanctifying work in our lives. This work of the Spirit leads to an active desire to embrace all of God's sovereign will with joy. Therefore, to learn to be content we must pray and ask God to produce contentment in our souls. If you look up the word *contentment* in a thesaurus, you find synonyms such as these: happy, satisfied, pleased, comfortable, at ease. Being content results from being satisfied with what God gives us, when and where he gives it, and why and how he gives it. Biblical contentment is an attitude of mind that displays complete confidence in God's total care in the midst of distressing, even devastating, circumstances. It evidences willing and genuine trust in God and his love and wisdom.

Contentment is a mix of the fruit of the Spirit: love, joy, peace, patience, and so on (see Gal. 5:22–23). Joy includes the kind of happiness that comes from having God as the object of its highest pleasure.

True happiness is a result of the Holy Spirit's sanctifying work. Please don't misunderstand—by happiness, I don't mean the kind of superficial good feelings we get when things go our way and we get what we want. Real happiness comes from wanting what God wants for us. It comes from being made increasingly holy through the Spirit's sanctifying work. Happiness and holiness are not opposites; they are two sides of the same coin. The work of the Spirit in our inner being produces a sweet kind of happiness that is contentment. The Spirit does this by teaching us to esteem God as the object of our greatest pleasure. When we seek God for who he is and grow in relationship with him, we increase our ability to be content and satisfied. "The young lions suffer want and hunger; but those who seek the LORD lack no good thing" (Ps. 34:10).

To reach the cruising altitude of contentment, the importance of managing our thoughts and setting our mind on the things above cannot be overstated.

> If then you have been raised with Christ, seek the things that are above, where Christ is, seated at the right hand of God. Set your minds on things that are above, not on things that are on earth. For you have died, and your life is hidden with Christ in God. . . . And let the peace of Christ rule in your hearts, to which indeed you were called in one body. And be thankful. Let the word of Christ dwell in you richly, teaching and admonishing one another in all wisdom, singing psalms and hymns and spiritual songs, with thankfulness in your hearts to God. And whatever you do, in word or deed, do everything in the name of the Lord Jesus, giving thanks to God the Father through him. (Col. 3:1–3, 15–17)

If we simply allow our mind to drift, it is likely we will be discontent because we live in a culture that breeds and feeds discontentment.

Contentment involves living so that we are not controlled by our circumstances. It means not being ruled by the situations in which we find ourselves. Pastor and theologian Philip Ryken provides us with this wise observation:

> As long as we base our sense of contentment on anything in the world, we will always find some excuse to make ourselves miserable. Our

problem is not on the outside—it's on the inside, and therefore it will never be solved by getting more of what we think we want. If we do not learn to be satisfied right now in our present situation—whatever it is—we will never be satisfied at all. . . . The truth is that if God wanted us to have more right now, we would have it. . . . If we were supposed to be in a different situation in life, we would be in it. Instead of always saying, 'If only this' and 'If only that,' God calls us to glorify him to the fullest right now. . . . Contentment means wanting what God wants for us rather than what *we* want for us. The secret to enjoying this kind of contentment is to be so satisfied with God that we are able to accept whatever he has or has not provided.[1]

The secret to contentment is being entirely satisfied with God and his provision for us. But what happens if we are not satisfied?

FALSE CONTENTMENT

Here is a partial list of ways that we, as widows, might attempt to find contentment if our relationship with God is not one of unreserved trust in his provision:

- *Escapism*: running away through entertainment, travel, people, a packed schedule.
- *Pseudo optimism*: faking contentment, being proud of always looking on the "bright side."
- *Fatalism*: attributing to fate the outcome of our lives resulting in lessened personal responsibility and denying the sovereign control of God.
- *Complacency*: a "what's the use" attitude that often leads to laziness.
- *Stoicism*: enduring suffering through personal resolve rather than dependence on God; allowing trials to deepen trust in self rather than in God.
- *Mere resignation*: settling for what God has brought into our lives rather than embracing it wholeheartedly.
- *Self-pity*: the pain that feels good because it enables us to keep our eyes on ourselves; it makes us feel noble and worthy of attention. It is pride in being a sufferer with the unspoken mantra "I deserve better."

None of these strategies brings true and lasting contentment. None of them honors God. Rather, they disparage our Lord because our reliance on them reveals that we believe him to be the source of our discontent rather than its solution. If Christ is not our contentment, then something else is—and that is idolatry. It means that something else is occupying the place that Jesus Christ ought to have in our life. We will never be content in widowhood if we pursue peace, joy, and satisfaction in anything but union with Christ.

DISCONTENTMENT

When we reflect on our circumstances in a grumbling, complaining manner, we are actually finding fault with God. That might not be our intent, but that's what we're doing. We often do not realize the serious nature of sinful discontentment. I do not mean that we cannot express to God and others a deep sadness in the loss of our spouse. Deep sorrow is appropriate and normal in the time of loss, but discontentment is not the same thing as godly sorrow.

Discontentment may smolder in us when we don't get what we expect out of life. This might be especially true of widows who lose their mate at a younger age. Becoming a "premature" widow can seem unfair and untimely. But such an outlook reveals the lack of an eternal perspective. My husband and I looked forward to living out the rest of our lives together, as my husband's grandfather and grandmother had. They were an endearing couple who lived into their mid-eighties and we loved spending time with them. I envisioned our future life full of friends, family, travel, and quiet moments together recalling precious memories. But God had different plans in mind for both of us. What I considered to be good for our future together was not what God chose for us. God did not give you or me the promise that our spouse would live to a ripe old age.

If we are not careful, we may draw wrong conclusions about God when our expectations are not met. Expectations are especially problematic when they become demands or requirements, whether spoken or unspoken. We expect that God will do what seems obviously best to us. Since we are without a spouse, we have a choice to make—accept the will of God with a submissive and joyful spirit or rebel against his will, dishonoring him and making ourselves miserable. Let us pray that we will quickly and gratefully yield to God's design for our lives. We must not ruin our testimony by being bitter, resentful, and discontented. Instead we can use this time to know God better and rest in his provision. "Satisfy us in the morning with your steadfast love, that we may rejoice and be glad all our days" (Ps. 90:14).

We must resist Satan's attempts to lure us into discontentment and all the potential grumblings of the flesh. Complaining is a major feature of discontentment, and it is always sin to complain about God or about anything he has done. His ways are perfect and often beyond our understanding, so they are not to be criticized by mere mortals like us. If we allow ourselves to be disappointed with God, we don't really possess a true knowledge of God or ourselves.

LEARNING CONTENTMENT IS A PROCESS

The apostle Paul said he had learned to be content. He didn't just wake up one day contented and satisfied with his life in Christ. He went through a process of being taught the truth, applying it to his life, and teaching others how to see everything from a heavenly perspective. That's what you and I need to do also. As with everything else about life in Christ, this learning process is only possible through the presence of the Holy Spirit in our lives. He is our teacher who guides us into the truth and gives us grace to embrace that truth wholeheartedly so that we can live above our circumstances.

We learn contentment by facing the reality of and thinking biblically about our situation. It's a contentment that flows from the vine into us, the branches (see John 15:1–11). The sap of godly contentment is always available to fill our spiritual veins. The sap will flow freely in us if there is:

- frequent confession of sin;
- meditation on God's Word;
- memorization of God's Word;
- trust in God for everything;
- heavenly mindedness;
- prayer guided by Scripture;
- ready acceptance of suffering as means to knowing God better.

God has given you and me a particular assignment to carry out in life, and therefore we should always interpret God's dealings with us in the best light. We must always assume that he is up to something good with us. When discontentment is troubling you, the way out is to seek the Lord.[2] Fight against restlessness and discontentment rather than giving in to those feelings.

One of the best encouragements toward contentment is to keep an eternal perspective on life. Read the book of Ephesians repeatedly to get this perspective, to get the big picture of what God is doing in the world.[3] God works all things according to the counsel of his will so that we might be to the praise of his glory. In her devotional book *Contentment: A Godly Woman's Adornment*, Lydia Brownback writes these inspiring words:

> When we look at God—among his people, in his Word, and by his Spirit—we are going to realize that the present is actually better than the past. It is better because God is the one who brought us where we are today. And the God who led us here is good, kind, and, let's not forget, purposeful. Everything he does in our lives, everywhere he leads us, is designed to fulfill his primary intention for us, which is to know him better. Contentment does not lie around the next corner. It is not waiting for us on the other side of today's difficulty, nor is it lost with yesterday. Contentment is where God is, and God is with us today.[4]

As we learn and exhibit contentment even in the face of widowhood, we manifest the power and love of God, who makes all things beautiful in his time.

> Jesus, my all in all thou art;
> my rest in toil, my ease in pain,
> the medicine of my broken heart,
> in war my peace, in loss my gain,
> my smile beneath the tyrant's frown,
> in shame my glory and my crown.[5]

15

REMEMBERING THE PAST

Say not, "Why were the former days better than these?"
For it is not from wisdom that you ask this.
ECCLESIASTES 7:10

The paintings of Charles Wysocki have delighted my heart for many years. They depict days gone by, some of them in places that hold memories for me. When I became a widow, I found particular interest in his series of paintings called "Ladies In Waiting."[1] Wysocki captures the pensive mood of women whose husbands are seafaring men gone for months or years upon the sea.

LOOKING BACK

My favorite painting in this series is entitled "I Hope Your Seas Are Calm, My Captain." For many years, my husband and his brother enjoyed boating together, an activity that provided them with lots of hilarious stories. When I look at this painting, I think of how my husband's seas are now entirely calm while mine are storm tossed. The captain's wife is painted standing alone on a widow's walk staring out to sea in the frozen winter air.[2] As a new widow, I looked intently at this painting because it summed up how I felt about my situation. Time seemed frozen as I stood looking at the past alone.

Much of the charm of Wysocki's paintings is the nostalgic feelings they can engender. Why are we humans prone to nostalgia? What makes the past sometimes seem better than the future? When we look at the past, we know how things turned out, and such knowledge makes us feel more in control. We tend to feel threatened by things that are beyond our con-

127

trol. In remembering, a widow often casts the best light on the past and therefore might forget the way things actually were.

In order to learn to remember rightly, let's look at Psalm 77. The psalmist, Asaph, is recalling his former happiness, lamenting over his present distress, and feeling sorry for himself (vv. 1–9). Then he shifts his focus onto God (vv. 10–20). Notice in the beginning of the psalm how many times Asaph refers to himself. He is pouring out his heart to God. He is not sleeping, and he is so distressed that he is beyond words. In days past, he has been happy in his walk with God but now his situation is different and God seems distant.

> I cry aloud to God,
>> aloud to God, and he will hear me.
> In the day of my trouble I seek the Lord;
>> in the night my hand is stretched out without wearying;
>> my soul refuses to be comforted.
> When I remember God, I moan;
>> when I meditate, my spirit faints.
> You hold my eyelids open;
>> I am so troubled that I cannot speak.
> I consider the days of old,
>> the years long ago.
> I said, "Let me remember my song in the night;
>> let me meditate in my heart."
>> Then my spirit made a diligent search:
> "Will the Lord spurn forever,
>> and never again be favorable?
> Has his steadfast love forever ceased?
>> Are his promises at an end for all time?
> Has God forgotten to be gracious?
>> Has he in anger shut up his compassion?" (vv. 1–9)

James Boice comments: "If we hurt, there is nothing wrong with expressing it and telling the Lord what we feel. But we must not stop there, rehearsing our disappointments endlessly. We need to move on, as the psalmist does."[3] Asaph asked himself questions that had the effect of leading him to proper thinking about his situation. And in the rest of the psalm, we see how Asaph moved on.

> Then I said, "I will appeal to this,
>> to the years of the right hand of the Most High."
> I will remember the deeds of the LORD;
>> yes, I will remember your wonders of old.
> I will ponder all your work,
>> and meditate on your mighty deeds.
> Your way, O God, is holy.
>> What god is great like our God?
> You are the God who works wonders;
>> you have made known your might among the peoples.
> You with your arm redeemed your people,
>> the children of Jacob and Joseph. (vv. 10–15)

Asaph says—"I will appeal," "I will remember" (twice), "I will ponder . . . and meditate." These "I wills" are all directed toward God, not himself. Asaph changed his focus from his inward experience outward toward God. Boice points out, "Earlier he was remembering the past and how wonderful it was compared to his grim present. In this stanza [verses 10–15] he is remembering God and his works, which makes all the difference."[4] Look at the things he remembers about God: his works/deeds, wonders, holiness, greatness, power, and faithfulness. We need to remember and meditate on these things too.

REMEMBER WHAT GOD HAS DONE FOR YOU

God always was, always is, and always will be sovereignly and lovingly in control of all that comes into your life. Because we are all sinners who deserve hell, the fact that God through his Son has chosen to save some and grant them eternal life with him in heaven is a mercy of the greatest magnitude. Reflect on his great love and mercy. Remember with the utmost gratitude his love that led to your salvation, his mercies that result in your provision and protection, his gifts of beloved family and friends. The latter are loaned to us for a time on this earth. When God decides to take them, he is exercising his full right to do so, and we have no claim on them.

We must accept that God has something new for us now and not stay stuck in the past. John Calvin put it this way: "If anyone looks back with a feeling of regret for the situation that he has abandoned, he cannot apply the whole bent of his mind to what he is engaged in."[5] By "abandoned," Calvin means a situation that you have had to leave behind. We must embrace the future knowing that God will be with us and that he is taking us in a direction that will display his glory and make us more like Christ. The same God who blessed you in the past will bless you in the present and the future. Remember the past in order to trust God for the present and the future.

SEEING FROM GOD'S PERSPECTIVE

When you want to go somewhere in your car, you don't stare in the rearview mirror. You concentrate on what is in front of you with only momentary glances at what is behind you. Learning to live as a widow is similar. If you spend too much time thinking about what is past, you will not be able to focus your mind and energy on what is ahead. Perhaps the future seems like a solid block wall. But, as Joshua found out at Jericho, God is an expert at making walls fall down.

Focus on what you have, not on what you do not have. God does not withhold good things from those who walk uprightly. In his book *Living the Cross Centered Life*, C. J. Mahaney observes about the apostle Paul:

> For Paul, the gospel—this "word of the cross"—was no cold theological formula. Paul lived a cross centered life because the cross had saved and transformed his own life. Paul never forgot what he once had been, or the mercy and grace God showed him. This remained at the forefront of his mind.[6]

By remembering what he had once been, Paul was able to focus on and be grateful for what he now possessed. He was effective in the present because he had God's perspective on his past.

REGRETS

We all say and do things we regret. We sin against others and we are sinned against by others. You may need to go to God and ask his forgiveness for some particular way you sinned against your spouse; do so, and then be free in Christ. Do not say that you cannot forgive yourself, for that would not be consistent with biblical teaching.[7] If you are truly repentant, God will forgive you, and that is the end of the issue. Accept his forgiveness and stop bringing up to yourself how you sinned against your deceased husband. God's forgiveness ends your guilt and sets you free to move on. When we linger over past wrongdoing, we are practicing unbelief because we are not trusting that the blood of Christ really cleanses us from all sin. We must go to the cross and remind ourselves of the provision that God has made for our sins to be forgiven.

Rest content that God will judge with perfect fairness what kind of wife you were. Paul counseled himself to leave the judgment of his actions to God:

> But with me it is a very small thing that I should be judged by you or by any human court. In fact, I do not even judge myself. For I am not aware of anything against myself, but I am not thereby acquitted. It is the Lord who judges me. Therefore do not pronounce judgment before the time, before the Lord comes, who will bring to light the things now hidden in darkness and will disclose the purposes of the heart. Then each one will receive his commendation from God. (1 Cor. 4:3–5)

Believe in God's merciful forgiveness of sin and go on in joy to serve him without the burden of regret. You cannot change the past, but you can give your concerns about it to God, knowing that he is a just judge. Your performance does not determine your final destiny; Christ's work on your behalf determines your destiny.

Once you have dealt with your regrets about the past, you may find it equally challenging not to dwell inordinately on the good things in the past. Brooding over the good that we've lost indicates how desperately we want to regain it. Emily Brontë's poem "Remembrance" is an excellent description of the pain of fond remembrance. Her words capture the tension between the pain of forgetting and the need to move on:

> Sweet Love of youth, forgive if I forget thee,
> While the world's tide is bearing me along:
> Sterner desires and other hopes beset me,
> Hopes which obscure, but cannot do thee wrong!

And referring to her soul, Brontë continues:

> And even yet I dare not let it languish,
> Dare not indulge in Memory's rapturous pain;
> Once drinking deep of that divinest anguish,
> How could I seek the empty world again?[8]

Brontë provides an apt description of remembering a deceased love.

I recall fearing the loss of memories, but I now realize it is inevitable that some of them will be lost. I also recall fearing that I would never stop remembering and would always feel the horrible depth of pain of losing my husband. I learned in this place between remembering and forgetting to seek out the peace and comfort that comes in fellowship with God. We can entrust to him our concerns and ask him to sustain us through this time. Ask the Spirit to teach you to appreciate where God has you now and to anticipate good times ahead with God. God does not waste our suffering. He will bring good out of it. So we rejoice in our sufferings because suffering produces endurance, endurance character, and character hope (Rom. 5:3–4).

HOW TO HONOR YOUR HUSBAND'S MEMORY

The wearing of wedding and engagement rings is a question that sometimes troubles widows. God will guide us about this and other concerns related to the transition from wife to widow. These are wisdom issues, not matters of right and wrong. The Scriptures do not directly address them.

There are, however, principles to follow from Scripture that can help guide us. One thing we must keep in mind is how our choices and actions will be perceived by those around us—how to be our "brother's keeper."[9] While we do not want to be ruled by fear of people's opinions, we need to minister to others and do things in a way that will communicate respect and honor regarding our late husband. Some widows wear their wedding rings for the rest of their lives, while others remove them after a time. For some widows, circumstances may necessitate the removal of his personal possessions soon after his death, while others have time to sort through things and give them away bit by bit. You may even want to save a few special items as keepsakes. What we surely want to avoid is changing nothing at all and making a shrine out of keeping everything exactly as it was for years on end.

Tell your grandchildren about their grandfather's life, and when discussing his death, use it as an opportunity to teach your grandchildren about heaven and hell, about the gospel of Jesus Christ, and about what God is doing in the world. You might want to make with them a memory book of their grandfather's life. Think of creative ways to remember with honor and with purpose the life of your husband.

A PROPER SORT OF BIBLICAL FORGETFULNESS

In the Scriptures we can observe the way God remembers his people—acknowledging the reality of their weaknesses but making the overall assessment of their lives a positive one. The Scriptures do not gloss over human weaknesses. But, in the end, what is the thing we most remember about David? He was a man after God's own heart. What do we remember about Abraham? He was a friend of God. About Peter? He was the rock on which the church was built as he boldly declared the gospel. The saints in Scripture were weak and sinful like us. However, the thing God chose to emphasize about their lives was their relationship to him.

In your remembrance of your husband, it is right to acknowledge that he was not perfect. He was a sinner, and not all aspects of his past were exemplary. But the overall impression of his life should be a positive remembrance. Dwell on the things that were fine and good about him while also recognizing his imperfections. It seems good to apply the Golden Rule—remember your husband in a way in which you yourself would want to be remembered.

Memories can be a blessing if we remember the way in which God remembers his people and follow his example. We can be set free from regrets and set the whole direction of our minds toward what God has for us today.

> Our God, our help in ages past,
> our hope for years to come,
> our shelter from the stormy blast,
> and our eternal home.[10]

STRETCHING FORWARD

*But one thing I do: forgetting what lies behind and straining forward
to what lies ahead, I press on toward the goal for the prize
of the upward call of God in Christ Jesus.*

PHILIPPIANS 3:13–14

One of my friends is a missionary appointee to Eastern Germany. Because she is staying with me until she leaves for Europe, I am able to observe how she is preparing to go. After receiving a clear call from God to this work, she is pouring every ounce of time and energy into getting ready to follow the Lord's leading. She is raising prayer and financial support by speaking at churches and visiting individual supporters. She is working with her sending church and the mission organization that is overseeing the work. And she is diligently studying the German language. Almost all her efforts are focused on that future work. She is stretching forward to reach the goal of taking the gospel to people who have little or no knowledge of it.

GETTING READY

What about you and me? What has God called us to now that our former call as godly wives is (at the present moment and perhaps for this life) no longer our calling? Do we have anything to stretch toward? Any goals to reach? Or are we simply going to squander the time we have? It's tempting to do nothing because doing anything takes energy, something which you may have very little of now. To counter the temptation, let's turn to the Scriptures and find direction for the future.

Imprisoned in Rome, the apostle Paul could have thrown up his hands and declared that his life had reached a standstill. Instead, he seized whatever opportunities came his way to tell others about Jesus Christ. I've found the letter that Paul wrote to the Philippians while he was in that Roman prison to be a pattern for living as a widow. The letter has much to say about the Christian life, but I want to pull out those things—some resolutions—that seem particularly helpful to widows as we face the future. I have never been one for New Year's resolutions, but, as a widow, I found it helpful to sketch out some resolutions to give my life direction. Think about what a resolution is: a formal expression of will or intent. In the diagram Mending by Intending are fifteen resolutions gleaned from the letter to the Philippians to apply as we stretch forward to glorify God in our widowhood.

MENDING BY INTENDING

	Verses from Philippians	**Resolution**
1.	What has happened to me should serve to advance the gospel (1:12).	I will pray about and look for ways to spread the gospel, especially among the bereaved.
2.	To live is Christ and to die is gain (1:21).	I will seek to love Christ more because the Lover of my soul *is* my life, and he is satisfying and exhilarating.
3.	If I am to live, that means fruitful labor for me (1:22).	I will not merely exist and waste my time; I will work to advance the honor of the kingdom of Christ in the world.
4.	Look not only to your own interests but also to the interests of others (2:4).	I will accept responsibility for myself and foster in myself true interest in the lives and concerns of others.
5.	Do all things without grumbling or questioning (2:14).	I will not be a complainer because I believe that what God gives to me or takes from me is out of his great love for me.
6.	Forget what lies behind and strain forward to what lies ahead (3:13).	I will stretch with eyes wide open toward the work God has for me now instead of living in the past.
7.	Press on toward the goal (3:14).	I will make every effort to know Christ and to imitate him, and I will look forward to being forever with him.
8.	Stand firm in the Lord (4:1).	I will plant my feet on the solid Rock of Christ and receive his power to remain faithful.
9.	Rejoice in the Lord always (4:4).	I will rejoice in the Lord at all times by gazing upon his beauty, enjoying his nearness, and praying with thanksgiving.

10.	Be reasonable/moderate knowing that the Lord is near (4:5).	I will exercise self-control so that I will be stable and even-tempered to the glory of God and the good of those around me.
11.	Don't give in to anxiety but instead pray (4:6).	I will walk by faith and cast my cares on the Lord by humbling myself before him.
12.	Keep your thoughts focused on Christ, his ways, and his works (4:8).	I will love God and his Word; reading daily and aiming to fill up my mind with God.
13.	Be content no matter the circumstances (4:11).	I will be grateful for whatever God gives me and stay close to him with a happy heart.
14.	Get your strength from your relationship with Christ (4:13).	I will depend on Christ to infuse into my soul the spiritual strength I need to live in a manner worthy of him.
15.	God will supply your needs (4:19).	I will trust God to supply all that I need for both my body and my soul.

I limited the number of my resolutions to keep the list workable, but if you'd like to, you could make your list longer by pulling more principles out of Philippians or another portion of Scripture. Be sure to tie your resolutions closely and faithfully to the text.

Of course, we won't implement these resolutions perfectly or wholly consistently. But they provide a target, a goal—something to shoot for. Aim for nothing and you'll get nothing; aim high and you will be pleasing to God. I find having a structured pattern like this motivating. Instead of letting life carry me along as one day gives way to another, I profit from the intentional effect these resolutions have on guiding my future.

SHIFTING GEARS

On the gearshift of life, there is no reverse. The only choice is to go forward. The good thing about this road trip is that God is in the driver's seat. He knows the way to where we are going, so we cannot get lost. But sometimes we *feel* like we're sitting on the side of the road in a disabled vehicle. It looks like life is passing us by. We see people around us speeding by with their lives. We wonder how they can do it when our lives have been brought to a screeching halt. We feel abandoned and alone. Living intentionally with biblically based resolutions to guide us like a road map can be a useful way to counter spiritual inertia. We can enter into the future confident of reaching our destination.

What if you don't want to go forward even after a lengthy period of time? If you find that you have an ongoing lack of desire to go forward, then perhaps it is time to try to discover the source of this immobilization. Is it possible that your husband was an idol in your life and that you worship the life you once had with him? I asked myself this question and found insight in these words by John Piper:

> *Enjoyment is becoming idolatrous when its loss ruins our trust in the goodness of God.* There can be sorrow at loss without being idolatrous. But when the sorrow threatens our confidence in God, it signals that the thing lost was becoming an idol.
>
> *Enjoyment is becoming idolatrous when its loss paralyzes us emotionally so that we can't relate lovingly to other people.* This is the horizontal effect of losing confidence in God. Again: great sorrow is no sure sign of idolatry. Jesus had great sorrow. But when desire is denied, and the effect is the emotional inability to do what God calls us to do, the warning signs of idolatry are flashing.[1]

When I lost my husband, I also lost an important role in life as his wife. I grieved over that loss. I prayed for grace to be willing to move on and embrace the new life that God was revealing to me. In order to stretch forward, we must leave the past behind and trust that what God has for us in the future will be fulfilling and enjoyable. It is vital to keep an eternal perspective on life or we will get lost in the details and not see the big picture. God is at work in our lives to bless us.

> So we do not lose heart. Though our outer self is wasting away, our inner self is being renewed day by day. For this light momentary affliction is preparing for us an eternal weight of glory beyond all comparison, as we look not to the things that are seen but to the things that are unseen. For the things that are seen are transient, but the things that are unseen are eternal. (2 Cor. 4:16–18)

God is sustaining us today and will sustain us tomorrow and all the rest of our days. He is at work renewing our inner being and preparing for us a glorious, eternal life with him.

What makes life worth getting out of bed in the morning? It is the person of Christ and the work he has given us to do. As we stretch forward, we want to be seeking God and desiring intimate fellowship with him. We want to be able to say with Paul that we desire to know God no matter what our circumstances are. As we go forward, we must grow in our affection for God. We must prefer God over anything else that competes for our affections.

Thomas Chalmers was a nineteenth-century preacher and teacher. In a sermon entitled, "The Expulsive Power of a New Affection," he explained that the most effective way of drawing our minds away from someone or something we should not or cannot have is to offer to the mind something even more captivating.[2] In order to move forward and face the future with hope and gladness, we must direct our minds to something of greater worth and excellence.

Chalmers's point is that we will go forward enthusiastically when we so love God that our love for him propels us onward and satisfies the depths of our soul. The person of Christ must so allure us that we are totally taken up with him. The pain of the loss of our husband begins to decrease as our love for Christ increases, widens, deepens, becomes *the* love of our life. Marriage as we know it is only a temporal state anyway. In heaven, the only marriage will be that between Christ and his people. Accordingly, as you go forward, let your happy singleness be a picture of what all Christians will experience in heaven at the marriage of the bride and the Lamb.

Elisabeth Elliot is known for saying, "Do the next thing."[3] In your struggle to go forward, if you can do nothing else, at least do the next thing. Wash the clothes, pay the bills, cook a nice meal (for yourself and, perhaps, to share with someone else), clean the house, call a friend who needs to hear your voice, and soon, as day follows day, you will be moving into the future. As you give up the past and move on serving Christ with enthusiasm, you will be able to look back on your new life with a sparkle in your eye. You will see the goodness and faithfulness of God as you walk with him and serve him.

Geoff Thomas, in his sermon on Philippians 3:13–14 entitled "The Marks of a Mature Christian," encourages us to pray this way: "Lord here is a new day given to me by you. Your mercies are new this morning. There are new things to be done, and new lessons to be learned. Help me to use this day properly as I head for home."[4]

HEAVEN BOUND

If you are going to step into all your tomorrows with hope, then you must keep your eyes focused heavenward. The Christian life is lived in between what you already possess of eternal life—which is knowing God and Jesus Christ ("This is eternal life, that they know you the only true God, and Jesus Christ whom you have sent," John 17:3)—and the ultimate goal of seeing the Lord face-to-face in heaven ("Beloved, we are God's children now, and what we will be has not yet appeared; but we know that when he appears we shall be like him, because we shall see him as he is," 1 John 3:2).

The psalmist Asaph expressed his desire to keep a heavenly perspective on life in this way: "Whom have I in heaven but you? And there is nothing on earth that I desire besides you. My flesh and my heart may fail, but God is the strength of my heart and my portion forever" (Ps. 73:25–26). If our *principal* motivation for wanting to go to heaven is anything other than desiring to see the Lord Jesus Christ face-to-face, then there is something amiss in our longing to go there.

In the New Testament letter to the Hebrews, we read that Christians who acknowledge that they are strangers and exiles on earth make it clear that "they desire a better country, that is, a heavenly one" (Heb. 11:16). And what will we see when we get there?

> You have come to Mount Zion and to the city of the living God, the heavenly Jerusalem, and to innumerable angels in festal gathering, and to the assembly of the firstborn who are enrolled in heaven, and to God, the judge of all, and to the spirits of the righteous made perfect, and to Jesus, the mediator of a new covenant, and to the sprinkled blood that speaks a better word than the blood of Abel. (Heb. 12:22–24)

While it is quite right to look forward to seeing departed loved ones when we get to heaven, the person whom we should desire most to see is the Lord Jesus Christ. For now, we are to keep our spiritual eyes wide open and focused on Christ so that we can see him with the eyes of faith. When we get to heaven, we won't need faith anymore. Faith will become sight. Heaven is his home and our home, and Christ has gone ahead to prepare a place for us.

Let not your hearts be troubled. Believe in God; believe also in me. In my Father's house are many rooms. If it were not so, would I have told you that I go to prepare a place for you? And if I go and prepare a place for you, I will come again and will take you to myself, that where I am you may be also. (John 14:1–3)

This is your future, dear sister. So get up each morning, meet with the Lord, and engage in fruitful labor for his kingdom. Before you know it, you and I will meet in heaven and rejoice over the splendor of the Lord.

One of the most encouraging books about heaven that I have read (and I have read a fair number of books on heaven!) is Joni Eareckson Tada's *Heaven: Your Real Home*. Discussing her desire to go home to heaven, Joni says:

I like earth. But my heart pumps for heaven. . . . I have a glorious home-sickness for heaven, a penetrating and piercing ache. I'm a stranger in a strange land, a displaced person with a fervent and passionate pain that is, oh, so satisfying. The groans are a blessing. . . . It's a good life, but I am looking forward to going home. I miss my home. I miss God.[5]

Let's press on with eyes gazing on Christ and do the kingdom work God has assigned us to do while we look forward to our eventual home-going. Be encouraged by these words of Paul to the Thessalonians:

Now may our Lord Jesus Christ himself, and God our Father, who loved us and gave us eternal comfort and good hope through grace, comfort your hearts and establish them in every good work and word. (2 Thess. 2:16–17)

When I stand before the throne,
dressed in beauty not my own,
when I see thee as thou art,
love thee with unsinning heart,
then, Lord, shall I fully know,
not till then, how much I owe.[6]

17

DISTRACTION AND DEVOTION

The woman who is unmarried, and the virgin, is concerned about the things of the Lord, that she may be holy both in body and spirit; but one who is married is concerned about the things of the world, how she may please her husband. This I say for your own benefit; not to put a restraint upon you, but to promote what is appropriate and to secure undistracted devotion to the Lord.

1 CORINTHIANS 7:34–35 NASB

My computer worktable sits in front of a double window that looks out onto the backyard. Beyond is a large park and hills off in the distance. Often, I am engrossed in my work and unaware of what is going on around me for considerable stretches of time. But then a helicopter flies overhead and I look up. The clouds are billowing in a pattern that looks like a giant castle. The bright, yellow marigolds blaze in the sun and the delicate, pink cosmos wave in the breeze. A robin is yanking a worm out of the ground, and the neighbor's cat is inching toward my bird feeder. I soon find myself, if I am not careful, wandering outside and seeing many things I need to do. One helicopter flying overhead and I've succumbed to distraction.

DON'T LOOK NOW BUT . . .

Loving God and living for him is the key to honoring him in widowhood. The way to be happy even in our sorrow is to gaze on Christ, to keep our eyes fixed on him in undistracted devotion, and to be about his kingdom work. Beware—the world, the flesh, and the Devil will oppose this kind of undistracted resolve in every possible way.

In the first letter to the Corinthians, the apostle Paul advised the church regarding some ways they might be distracted from devotion to God. Whether Paul was concerned about the distractions of persecution or the distractions presented by a wrong understanding of marriage among the Corinthians or both, he wanted them to realize the importance of concentrating their attention on God.

Certainly there are legitimate distractions, and that includes those that accompany the marriage relationship. Paul mentions this in his discussion about marriage, pointing out that the duties attached to it distract the Christian from the ability to focus exclusively on God. Distractions, whether right or wrong ones, lessen our capacity for focusing on the things above. Additionally, a myriad of distracting elements in our culture vie for our attention and weaken our resolve to be fully devoted to the Lord. Being distracted from concentrating on the Lord himself is nothing new.

MARTHA AND MARY

The story of Martha and Mary is found in Luke's Gospel. When Martha's name is raised in Christian circles, she seems to be remembered more for this incident than for her faithful confession to Christ after her brother, Lazarus, died. First, we'll look at the incident describing her distractedness and then we'll observe her in her finest recorded moment.

> Now as they were traveling along, He [Jesus] entered a village; and a woman named Martha welcomed Him into her home. She had a sister called Mary, who was seated at the Lord's feet, listening to His word. But Martha was distracted with all her preparations; and she came up *to Him* and said, "Lord, do You not care that my sister has left me to do all the serving alone? Then tell her to help me." But the Lord answered and said to her, "Martha, Martha, you are worried and bothered about so many things; but *only* one thing is necessary, for Mary has chosen the good part, which shall not be taken away from her." (Luke 10:38–42 NASB).

We see Martha in a different light in the Gospel of John. John writes that Jesus went to Bethany after the death of his friend Lazarus, the brother of Mary and Martha:

Now Jesus loved Martha and her sister and Lazarus. So when Martha heard that Jesus was coming, she went and met him, but Mary remained seated in the house. Martha said to Jesus, "Lord, if you had been here, my brother would not have died. But even now I know that whatever you ask from God, God will give you." Jesus said to her, "Your brother will rise again." Martha said to him, "I know that he will rise again in the resurrection on the last day." Jesus said to her, "I am the resurrection and the life. Whoever believes in me, though he die, yet shall he live, and everyone who lives and believes in me shall never die. Do you believe this?" She said to him, "Yes, Lord; I believe that you are the Christ, the Son of God, who is coming into the world." (John 11:5, 20–27)

My point in looking at these two portions of Scripture is to demonstrate that even a godly woman like Martha who loved the Lord and believed deeply that he was the Messiah could in a weak moment of distraction fail to honor the Lord she loved. Even after the death of her beloved brother, which Jesus did not prevent, Martha made her solid confession of belief in Christ as the Son of God. Martha ought to be remembered primarily for this confession of belief in Jesus Christ rather than for her momentary lapse into distracted, impatient criticism. We do, however, want to learn from both these incidents.

Referring to Martha's words to Jesus after her brother's death, Leon Morris makes the following observations:

> These words of Martha do not always receive the attention they should. . . . With all of her faults, Martha was a woman of faith and hers was a significant declaration. . . . Her faith is not a vague, formless credulity. It has content, and doctrinal content at that. . . . Taken together [her] affirmations give us as high a view of the person of Christ as one well may have. Martha should be remembered by this moving declaration rather than by her worst moment of criticism and fretfulness.[1]

Martha was distracted at times but she was thoroughly devoted to Jesus, as was her sister, Mary. Martha and Mary do not appear in the Scriptures to give us pictures of psychological types, as has been suggested by some authors. Rather, the stories of these sisters and their friends show how

Jesus interacted with his disciples, teaching them the truth about himself and themselves and strengthening their faith. We see both their weaknesses and their strengths and can identify those same things in ourselves.

When we are distracted from loving Christ and fixing our eyes on him, we need to hear the admonition to Martha as an admonition to ourselves: you are worried and bothered about many things; but only one thing is necessary. Choose the good part, which shall not be taken away from you. Choose the good part—of being careful to spend time at Jesus' feet, in his Word, getting to know him intimately and therefore loving him with less distraction.

SPIRITUAL A.D.D.

Minimizing unnecessary distractions is something all Christians need to do in order to be devoted to God. What are the particular distractions that may enter in or intensify during widowhood? How do we attend to God and ignore the onslaught of twenty-first-century distractions? In the midst of grief, it is oh, so tempting to take what seems to be the easy path. Weary from constantly having to adjust to life without our spouse, it seems easy—and comforting—to find some way to simply escape from grief.

Such escapes usually come through the excessive use of or appeal to certain things or people. It's easy to understand how a widow might be tempted to spend many hours watching television or videos. A good story, especially when presented to an active imagination, can take the mind away to another place. Watching a film for a couple of hours may bring relief from the relentless silence of being alone. When I tried that, I received a harsh jolt when the film was over and I crashed back into the reality of my loss and pain.

Food can also be used as a distraction from the pain of grief. Whenever we are depressed, sad, or disappointed, we might be tempted to use food as a source of consolation and distraction. Chocolate, right? The food of choice for those in a low mood—and it works. But how much, and for how long, and how often are we going to turn to food to try to quiet our restless, grieving souls? The Bible directs us in this way: "So, whether you eat or drink, or whatever you do, do all to the glory of God" (1 Cor. 10:31). "Happy are you, O land, when your king is the son of the nobility, and your princes feast at the proper time, for strength, and not for drunken-ness!" (Eccles. 10:17). Eating well is a hard thing for many women. We need to pray and ask our heavenly Father to give us such a strong desire for Christ that our desire to eat improperly will be extinguished by this greater affection for the Lord.[2] Ask God to give you more of Christ in your heart so that through him your comfort will overflow.

When we are under the pressure of bereavement, it's tempting to either idolize or ignore relationships with the people closest to us. We may ignore people who are a challenge but cling improperly to those with whom we are comfortable and whom we think can give us relief from our situation. Having dear friends to lean on is a gift from God, but we must take care that we do not look to them for the kind of support that can only come from the Lord. We must not let the temptation of loneliness cause us to use our friends in selfish ways. It's fine to pour out your heart to a dear friend, but if you do not also pour out your heart to the Lord and find solace in his presence, then you are putting your friend in the place of the Lord, and that is idolatry.

In Psalm 16 we find wise counsel from David concerning the focus of our lives. This psalm demonstrates undistracted devotion to the Lord:

> Preserve me, O God, for in you I take refuge.
> I say to the LORD, "You are my Lord;
>   I have no good apart from you."
> As for the saints in the land, they are the excellent ones,
>   in whom is all my delight.
> The sorrows of those who run after another god shall multiply;
>   their drink offerings of blood I will not pour out
>   or take their names on my lips.
> The LORD is my chosen portion and my cup;
>   you hold my lot.
> The lines have fallen for me in pleasant places;
>   indeed, I have a beautiful inheritance.
> I bless the LORD who gives me counsel;
>   in the night also my heart instructs me.
> I have set the LORD always before me;
>   because he is at my right hand, I shall not be shaken. (vv. 1–8)

This psalm has a thoroughly Godward focus. David says that the Lord is his portion. He demonstrates continual focus on God that leads to unshakable confidence in God. Verse 4 cautions us against pursuing those people or things that we may be tempted to set up as gods in our lives. If we do so, the result will be multiplied sorrow.

Children and grandchildren can be a significant blessing in your widowhood, but take note of how much and in what ways you depend upon them. Remember that they are grieving too. They have lost their father and grandfather. Be careful that you are not selfishly looking for comfort from them while ignoring their own need for comfort. Do not expect your children to become your single source of social contact. Do not use them as distractions from your loneliness. If you did not develop and cultivate friendships with your peers before the death of your husband, you will need to do that now.

RELATIONSHIP EXTREMES

Sometimes I feel like a woolly mammoth that was frozen in ice for millennia but now has been thawed out to return to life on earth. A widow's life changes drastically, and this will affect her friendships. Some friendships will be strengthened and others may fade away. Early in your widowhood it is likely that your friends will be the initiators of contact, but as time goes on, you may find that you will need to reach out to them. We must be willing to do this even if it takes considerable effort. It is all too easy to let feelings of sadness and sapped strength distract us from pursuing godly, mature friendships. We are one body in Christ, and we need each other, especially to spur one another on to love and good deeds.[3]

Friendships with couples change after the death of a spouse. Some will endure and some will not. In the ones that endure, make it a point to engage both wife and husband in conversation. Maintaining such a balance is important. Be aware of your eye contact and the expressions on your face. In other words, observe yourself. This shouldn't involve a huge burden of self-policing, but do be aware of how you are coming across to them. You want to minister love and grace to both of them. You want to rejoice in their ongoing marriage relationship and continue to be their friend so that you will do good to them and God will be glorified.

A widow who seeks to secure undistracted devotion to the Lord can be an effective witness to the majestic power, wisdom, and love of God. Losing a spouse is one of the most stressful events of life. If we crumble under the grief of it, what message are we sending to those around us? How can we build up the body of Christ if we do not demonstrate the sufficiency of God in these circumstances? If we run to false sources of comfort, do we realize how damaging that is to our testimony as Christians? Run instead to the true Comforter—to the one who alone is able to keep you from falling. Our Lord is able and willing to uphold all who trust in him. May we be faithful to fix our eyes on him in undistracted devotion.

> Jesus, thou joy of loving hearts,
> thou fount of life, thou light of men,
> from the best bliss that earth imparts
> we turned unfilled to thee again.
>
> Our restless spirits yearn for thee,
> wher-e'er our changeful lot is cast;
> glad when thy gracious smile we see,
> blest when our faith can hold thee fast.[4]

MAKING IMPORTANT DECISIONS

He leads the humble in what is right,
and teaches the humble his way. . . .
Who is the man who fears the LORD?
Him will he instruct in the way that he should choose.

PSALM 25:9, 12

Amelia Bedelia is one of my granddaughter's favorite storybook characters. Amelia, the housemaid, gets herself into all sorts of predicaments because she misunderstands directions. Her misinterpretations of her employers' orders lead to hilarious antics. We laugh at Amelia literally dressing in clothing a chicken that was supposed to be prepared for dinner or hanging lightbulbs on a clothesline when she was simply asked to turn out the lights.[1] But in real life, if we misunderstand God's directions and misapply them, it isn't funny. Instead, we find ourselves making poor decisions and reaping the unpleasant consequences.

GAINING WISDOM

A state of bereavement is one of the most difficult times in which to make important decisions. Grieving for your spouse puts an enormous strain on the mind. Decisions involve choices. We choose among options and make a determination of what we think is best. Choosing wisely includes considering the consequences our choices will bring. One of the manifestations of God's mercy is that his Word can make us wise for all things that pertain to life and godliness (2 Pet. 1:3). The book of Proverbs, in particular, teaches us about wisdom, as does the letter of James. "If any of you lacks wisdom, let him ask God, who gives generously to all without reproach, and it will be given him" (James 1:5). But all of Scripture, if understood and applied rightly, can guide us in making all manner of decisions. With the Holy Spirit as our guide, we can find either direct guidance or guidance that is extracted from principles laid out in his Word.

Let's briefly consider a few aspects of how we ought to implement decision making. For help I turn again and again to Arthur Pink's book *The Nature of God*.[2] The chapter entitled "The Guidance of God" is a treasure trove of wisdom regarding decision making. If you consider yourself weak or inexperienced in making decisions, you might also want to peruse some of the books in the suggested reading list.

Pink indicates three main means of obtaining guidance from God. First, consult the Word of God. A thorough search of the Scriptures will yield both explicit and implicit guidance. Be sure to employ sound interpretation as you study. Ask your pastor or consult a good commentary for help if you are uncertain of the meaning of a text. Second, pray for guidance from the Holy Spirit through his Word. Remember that one of the ministries of the Holy Spirit is to guide his people into the truth (see John 14, 15, and 16). He will lead you, teach you, and enable you to understand how to apply his Word to your decision-making process. Third, observe carefully how God is working in your circumstances. This includes seeking the counsel of those you trust. Ask for advice from people who have wisdom and knowledge in the area in question. "Without counsel plans fail, but with many advisers they succeed" (Prov. 15:22).

In spiritual matters, we do well to seek guidance from mature, wise, biblically well-informed Christians. When I say "spiritual matters," I am not simply referring to particular issues about the Bible or church. Spiritual matters can include many aspects of life: emotional, social, behavioral, relational, intellectual, vocational, and so on. Even many medical concerns have spiritual components to them. Unless we are facing an emergency, we should never make an important decision in haste but wait until we are reasonably sure of what we ought to do. We should most definitely avoid making decisions in the middle of the night. Things look different and usually somewhat better in the morning. Now let's consider briefly some areas in which widows need wisdom.

FINANCES

Unless you are proficient in financial matters, you may wish to seek help with financial decisions. It is crucial to find someone competent who is mainly concerned for your interests. Ask your pastor if he can refer you to a financial professional. Even if you hire an adviser, however, you will need to educate yourself to some extent about finances. As widows we need to be able to interact with and assess intelligently the advice we receive.

HEALTH

Medical decisions are multifaceted. Opinions in the medical community vary. To be informed medical consumers, we need to search diligently for accurate information, keeping in mind that a medical professional is a well-educated consultant. We make the final decision on what treatment we want if any. A competent, caring practitioner will not be offended if we pursue a second opinion, ask good questions, or follow information gleaned from other responsible sources.

Take someone with you to a medical appointment. A friend can be an extra pair of ears to help you remember what was said. Write down your questions and concerns and give your friend a copy. Decide ahead of time whether you want your friend to remind you of anything on the list you might forget to mention during the appointment. God calls us to be good stewards of our bodies, so be willing to do your homework and to interact wisely with those you choose for your care (see 1 Cor. 6:19–20; 1 Tim. 4:8).

HOUSING

I was at a Christmas party several years ago and found myself in a conversation with an elderly widow who lives in an upscale retirement community. Knowing that I was recently widowed, she appeared to want to take me under her wing and give me some advice. Eager to hear some words of wisdom, I listened closely as she began to speak. "Do you plan to stay in your home or are you going to move?" she asked. "I'm not sure," I replied. "I've barely had time to consider it." In hushed tones and with a knowing look, she then told me what happens after the lights are dimmed at the community where she lives. As she described the clandestine maneuvers she had observed, I felt myself becoming slightly sick as my mind pictured aged paramours stealthily entering one another's apartments. Please don't misunderstand. I'm not at all opposed to the faithful and loving expression of "married" sexuality at any age. But that's not the sort of sexual expression she was talking about.

Each retirement community has its own distinct social atmosphere. It is important to discern the general tone and whether it is a good fit for you. Some communities are affordable only for the wealthy, but there are others available for those of more modest means. National corporations manage most communities but some are affiliated with various religious denominations. If you are considering moving to elder housing, you need to investigate your options carefully. A personal visit to the community is essential to a good decision. Even if you can't afford it, visit any community that has a good reputation. You will likely come away with observations and materials that will provide valuable information in assessing the various options. Alternatively, you may decide to stay in your home and, if you need it, receive home care from an agency provider. Carefully check their credentials as well.

As we know, the likelihood of needing medical care increases as we age. If you are hospitalized while living in a continuing care retirement community (CCRC) and must be discharged to a skilled nursing unit (SNU), you have priority status for admission to the unit at your community. In such situations you will already be familiar with the quality of care and some of the caregivers. If you live at home and are hospitalized and then discharged straight to a SNU, you may have to accept placement, either temporary or permanent, in a facility that would not be your first choice. I have observed both situations with members of my extended family. It is possible to enter a CCRC too early and have a difficult adjustment made even more challenging. Most residents of retirement communities range in age from the middle fifties to over one hundred years old with the average age being in the late seventies and early eighties. If you are in relatively good health and can still maintain your home, a move to a retirement community when you are in the lower range of the age spread may seem premature. You could have a difficult time feeling like you fit in. But it seems to me that adjusting will be even harder if you wait too long. The longer we wait, the more chance there is of finding ourselves pressured to make a decision. And think about needing to sort through your belongings, packing up what you want to take, preparing the house for sale, and then moving. It is a daunting process at any age but extremely challenging when elderly and even more so when we must do it alone. (See Appendix 1 for thoughts on moving in with children.)

HOME MAINTENANCE

If you are going to stay in your home, you will likely need some help with home maintenance. I've found that asking for recommendations from men in my church who are building contractors or tradesmen has worked out well. Ask around your neighborhood and see if there are responsible young people who might want to do some jobs for you such as mowing grass and shoveling snow. Some churches provide help with light home maintenance through diaconal or intergenerational ministries. One church with which I am familiar has a sign-up sheet for anyone needing help with grass mowing, leaf raking, or snow removal. The youth group together with the deacons serve the older people in the congregation through these services.

TRANSPORTATION

Car maintenance is a challenge for me. Aside from turning the key in the ignition, I'm a dunce in the garage. The first time I put windshield washer fluid in the tank under the hood I had visions of becoming a race car driver. For help with maintaining your vehicle, ask people at your church for names of reliable mechanics, auto body workers, and tire companies. If your car is no longer under warranty, you might want to find an independent mechanic rather than taking your car back to the dealership. Dealer repairs are almost always more expensive. Five months after my husband died, the lease on my car expired. I decided not to purchase the car, which meant I needed to shop for a new one. One of my husband's favorite things was car shopping; consequently I left those decisions to him. I was, however, able to find help on the Internet at consumer Web sites. Armed with pricing information and accompanied by my car-savvy sister, I purchased a new car.

SECOND MARRIAGES

In a moment of cynical jesting with some friends, I said that I would not consider marrying again unless I could do an FBI background check on any potential mate. My husband and I met in high school, and our extended families lived for several generations in neighboring communities. My father worked for many years at a company that also employed my husband's grandfather. Due to those close connections, I was certain when I married that my husband was a person of good character. Personal knowledge of his family history gave me perspective and a context that aided my decision to marry him.

The Scriptures guide us on the topic of second marriages, especially 1 Corinthians 7. Regarding Paul's advice to widows in verses 39 and 40, Matthew Henry observes:

> It is certain, from this passage, that second marriages are not unlawful; for then the widow could not be at liberty to marry whom she pleased, nor to marry a second time at all. But the apostle asserts she has such a liberty, when her husband is dead, only with a limitation that *she marry in the Lord.* In our choice of relations, and change of conditions, we should always have an eye to God. Note, marriages are likely to have God's blessing only when they are made in the Lord, when persons are guided by the fear of God, and the laws of God, and act in dependence on the providence of God, in the change and choice of a mate—when they can look up to God, and sincerely seek his direction, and humbly hope for his blessing upon their conduct. *But she is happier,* says the apostle, *if she so abide* (that is, continue a widow) *in my judgment; and I think I have the Spirit of God,* v. 40. At this juncture, at least, if not ordinarily, it will be much more for the peace and quiet of such, and give them less hindrance in the service of God, to continue unmarried. And this, he tells them, was by inspiration of the Spirit. "Whatever your false apostles may think of me, I think, and have reason to know, that I have the Spirit of God." Note, change of condition in marriage is so important a matter that it ought not to be made but upon due deliberation, after careful consideration of circumstances, and upon very probable grounds, at least, that it will be a change to advantage in our spiritual concerns.[3]

What wonderful advice! Please read Henry's words again and let them sink into your mind if you are contemplating marriage.

As was noted in chapter 2, if a widow marries she must marry a Christian. Henry points out that a widow's decision to marry must be based on a concern for spiritual advancement. In other words, the principal reason to marry is that marrying a particular person will make both the widow and her new husband better able to glorify God and serve his kingdom. Together you must seek to grow in grace and knowledge of the Lord Jesus Christ. Otherwise, it is better to remain single. Referring to this same section of Scripture, D. A. Carson says, "Unlike pagans and secularists, we cannot make our chief joy turn on marriage, prosperity, or any other temporal thing. . . . There are responsible ways for Christians to enjoy these things . . . but *never* as if these things are ultimate."[4]

Marrying in an effort simply to get our personal needs met is biblically illegitimate because it is selfish and self-focused. Marriage is an opportunity to minister love and grace to our spouse, not to use him to get what we think we need.

GOD'S FAITHFULNESS

God wants us to know his will for our lives. He has revealed his will in his Word. Be assured that he will never lead you in a way that is inconsistent with the Scriptures. Diligently follow what is clear to you from the Scriptures, and God will reveal what is less clear in his own time. Pray and ask God to make his will plain to you in areas that seem filled with confusion. If you are obedient and humble, he will lead you to walk in the way he wants you to go. "Trust in the LORD with all your heart; do not depend on your own understanding. Seek his will in all you do, and he will direct your paths" (Prov. 3:5–6 NLT).

> All the way my Savior leads me, cheers each winding path I tread,
> gives me grace for ev-'ry trial, feeds me with the living bread.
> Though my weary steps may falter, and my soul a-thirst may be,
> gushing from the rock before me, lo, a spring of joy I see;
> gushing from the rock before me, lo, a spring of joy I see.[5]

NUMBERING YOUR DAYS WITH WISDOM

So teach us to number our days
that we may get a heart of wisdom. . . .
Satisfy us in the morning with your steadfast love,
that we may rejoice and be glad all our days.

PSALM 90:12, 14

Of all the chapters in this book, this one is the hardest for me to write. You, dear reader, are in the throes of bereavement, so why would I want to raise issues dealing with the end of *your* life? Can't these things wait until you are done with grieving? I earnestly wish they could. Moreover, if you are at all like me, your grieving will lessen but it will never go away completely. But facing the practical necessities surrounding your life's end cannot be long postponed. If you find this chapter too difficult to read at present, skip it and read it at a later time. But please do come back to it. I want the best for you, and handling these matters efficiently and wisely will help to ensure a better future.

THE BREVITY OF LIFE

Surely widows understand better than most people that life is short. Even though the reality of an empty house may provide fresh evidence every day, still, at times it is hard to believe that our husband is gone. Where did the time go? How swiftly it all passed by and how cruelly we miss his love. In Psalm 90, the words of Moses address the brevity of life:

> The years of our life are seventy,
> or even by reason of strength eighty;

> yet their span is but toil and trouble;
>> they are soon gone, and we fly away. . . .
> So teach us to number our days
>> that we may get a heart of wisdom. . . .
> Satisfy us in the morning with your steadfast love,
>> that we may rejoice and be glad all our days. (Ps. 90:10, 12, 14)

Verse 12 says, "Teach us." We need wisdom from God that will guide us in the use of our days. Rather than sit back and simply wait out our remaining days, we need to seek God's will. It saddens me when I hear of a widow who lacks the desire to continue her work in the kingdom of God.[1] Her spouse's purpose on this earth has ended, but hers has not.

ORDER HONORS GOD

When life seems good, or at least smooth enough to lull us into apathy regarding our eternal destination, we get comfortable with the way things are and lose our longing for a better country—a heavenly one. But the death of our spouse jars that indifference, and we come face-to-face with the brevity of life on this earth. Now that our life partner is not here to keep us company, share our joys and sorrows, and be our support in life's storms, we are better suited to accept the fact that we too will someday be gone. For the Christian woman who has trained herself to be heavenly minded, this fact will not shock her but remind her to get her house in order. Without her husband to care for her at life's end, she will need to plan for alternate means of support. This requires that certain legal and personal matters be pursued.

It is important that we not let too much time pass after the death of our spouse before attending to necessary legal and personal matters. Doing so will produce three good effects: (1) it will honor God;[2] (2) it will bless our descendants; and (3) it will give us peace of mind.

I am not an attorney, so I am by no means seeking to offer legal advice. I simply want to point out the value of having legal documents that will speak for us if we are no longer able to speak for ourselves. It is easy to delay addressing these issues. Time, expense, and inertia provoke us to drag our heels, so we must pray for the desire and the diligence to pursue the construction and completion of these necessary documents.

My experience has shown me that we ought to hire the best estate attorney we can afford. It will be money well spent. It is essential that we have a will. If we had a will before our husband died, it is necessary to update it to reflect the change in our marital status. Even if we are of modest means, a well-crafted will can spare our descendants a lot of headaches and protect our assets. Besides a will, it is important to have a document regarding healthcare decisions, such as a durable power of attorney (DPA). The term durable power of attorney refers to someone designated to speak and act on our behalf when we cannot speak or act for ourselves because of some mental or physical incapacity. Our DPA becomes our agent or proxy (substitute). You may also need a durable power of attorney for finance, a document to address your financial affairs.

Healthcare Decisions

Because end-of-life health care is sometimes, perhaps even often, riddled with complex decisions and difficult choices, we want to have in place a document that will work for us, not against us. We must think twice before signing any healthcare document that asks us to check off items on a list of possible medical interventions or treatments. We cannot adequately know today what will be the best options in a future health crisis. It is better to have a flexible document in which we name a healthcare proxy to make decisions for us, and in the process we should choose someone we trust who will be able to function well, if need be, under pressure from doctors, hospital staff, and insurers.

It is wise to discuss with our proxy our thoughts concerning medical or financial decisions. The best proxy will know us well and understand our values and beliefs. He or she will be able when needed to assess our situation and make the decision we would make if we could. Good preparation with our proxy includes issues such as the use of ventilators, resuscitation, transplants, and dialysis. It is never easy to have such conversations, but it is important. We must not avoid it. To help you think about these things, I have listed some resources in the Suggested

Reading—and do not overlook the Scriptures as you seek wisdom for these issues and decisions. Though the Bible is not a medical textbook, it provides us with principles from which we can glean wisdom to know how to think about life and its earthly end.

We can, with the help of our attorney, write our own medical proxy document. I did this with my estate attorney, and I included a page of biblical affirmations that guide my healthcare proxy in making decisions for me.[3] A well-constructed healthcare document may prevent a medical decision nightmare. While it is good to appreciate the many blessings of modern medicine, it is wise to be aware that medical procedures are not always helpful or desirable.

While there is no perfect answer to how to handle these difficult medical situations, we can increase the probability of a good outcome. We can educate ourselves, create the best documents we can, and communicate to responsible, trusted people our beliefs and desires should the occasion arise when we cannot speak for ourselves.

Financial Decisions

If we become incapacitated, we will need someone to pay our bills and transact other necessary business. This person is our finance proxy. Again, trustworthiness is key. Our proxy will need access to our personal financial information—the location of checkbooks, bank accounts, safety deposit box, and other paperwork, as well as contact information for our attorney and financial adviser. If we engage in online banking or stock trading, the proxy will need to know our passwords.

Funeral Plans

We can help our family by writing down our preferences for our funeral service, including the location (a church or funeral home), Scripture texts we want read, hymns or anthems, the names of service participants, and so on. Making such arrangements relieves our family of a lot of decisions. If arrangements went smoothly with your husband's funeral, you know the importance of doing so for your surviving family members. You can bless them by taking these decisions off their shoulders.

Leaving a Written Legacy

Sometimes people write what is called an "ethical will." This will is not a legal document; rather, it explains your beliefs and the worldview you adopted in living your life. It may also contain a family history and thoughts to be passed on to remaining family members. It could be written in the form of an autobiography. You could include a testimony of how you came to believe in the Lord Jesus Christ as your Savior and Lord. A written testimony could be a significant blessing to your family for generations.

ACCEPTING HELP GRACIOUSLY

Depending on the state of our health, we might need to ask for help with various things. Asking for help can be difficult. We prefer to think of ourselves as self-sufficient and independent. Some are stubborn and never ask for help. The key to avoiding difficulty here is to pray that God will give us the ability to honestly and humbly assess our situation and, if need be, to acknowledge our need for help. God can keep us from the self-deceit that keeps us from what we really need.

Unless we move every few years, it is surprising how blind we are to the amount of stuff that we accumulate. I've lived in my present home for over twenty-five years. It has limited storage space, which is an advantage. Instead of stockpiling and saving things, I've had to keep sorting and getting rid of whatever I don't use on a regular basis. The shortage of storage space has had the effect of making me generous in giving to those in need and of stifling the temptation to buy on impulse. My first thought when shopping (after considering the price of an item) concerns where I will store it.

We must not let either our house or our person get into poor condition because we are too proud to ask for help or to accept it when it is offered. We must guard against taking offense when someone offers to help. Since love assumes the best, we should assume good motives on the part of someone trustworthy, believing that the offer of help stems from love, care, and concern.

I've learned the value of traveling lightly through life, not keeping hold of a lot of unnecessary things. I have a friend who startled me one day by saying, half jokingly, that many of the things we have accumulated will end up at a garage sale someday. Her statement provided instant perspective for me. I realized that I could help my family by giving away superfluous items instead of leaving them with a monumental clean-up job. As a result, I spent several months emptying out the attic and basement and thinning out the remainder of the house.

It is also important to take care what we leave behind. I heard a man say that finding his deceased mother's diary was depressing because it was filled with all manner of complaints about her life. What will our heirs find after we are gone? We do well to get rid of whatever is nonessential and might prove hurtful or problematic, especially for siblings. We will not be around to explain what they find. We do not want to cause them discord. If there is something that must be divulged, we best do it now while we are able to explain it.

Our children might offer to help us, and if they do, we should accept their offer. In his first letter to Timothy, the apostle Paul gave instructions on how various groups within the church were to be treated, and he included the obligation that children and grandchildren have to care for the widows in their family:

> But if a widow has children or grandchildren, let them first learn to show godliness to their own household and to make some return to their parents, for this is pleasing in the sight of God. . . . But if anyone does not provide for his relatives, and especially for members of his household, he has denied the faith and is worse than an unbeliever. . . . If any believing woman has relatives who are widows, let her care for them. (1 Tim. 5:4, 8, 16)

If we refuse their help, we are denying them the opportunity to obey the instruction of the Lord. On the other hand, we would certainly not want to misuse these verses in 1 Timothy as a way to pressure our family into helping more than they are able.

In the past I have been blessed by people who helped me and by others who allowed me to help them. As they graciously accepted my help, I was touched by their humility. Getting to know people better by being in their home and helping where necessary allowed me to learn from them. I listened to their happy stories and also tales of hard times. I even learned how to do some chores better as they instructed me how they wanted them done. So when asking for help, we can be specific, describing what needs to be done and approximately how long it will take to complete. And we must remember to ask far enough in advance so our helpers can find time in their schedules to help us.

As we do our best to prepare, we remember that God is sovereign over the way our life ends. Psalm 116:15 says, "Precious in the sight of the Lord is the death of his saints." When we think that God "did not spare his own Son" but gave him up for us, we can be assured that he will be close to us in our greatest trial (see Rom. 8:32). "Neither death nor life . . . will be able to separate us from the love of God in Christ Jesus our Lord" (Rom. 8:38–39). Therefore, we can reject fear, get all our documents and personal belongings in order, and continue in faithful service to the Lord until he takes us home.

> All the way my Savior leads me—O the fullness of his love!
> Perfect rest to me is promised in my father's house above:
> when my spirit, clothed, immortal, wings its flight to realms of day,
> this my song through endless ages: Jesus led me all the way;
> this my song through endless ages: Jesus led me all the way![4]

LEARNING FROM YOUR WIDOWHOOD

Therefore, preparing your minds for action, and being sober-minded,
set your hope fully on the grace that will be brought to you at the
revelation of Jesus Christ.

1 PETER 1:13

In John's Gospel we find an event in which the disciples made a wrong assumption about what God was doing:

> As [Jesus] passed by, he saw a man blind from birth. And his disciples asked him, "Rabbi, who sinned, this man or his parents, that he was born blind?" Jesus answered, "It was not that this man sinned, or his parents, but *that the works of God might be displayed in him.* We must work the works of him who sent me while it is day; night is coming, when no one can work. As long as I am in the world, I am the light of the world." (John 9:1–5)

Later, after Jesus had healed the blind man and given him sight, the man confessed Jesus to be the Son of God and worshiped him (verse 38).

As widows, we need to guard against making wrong assumptions about what God is doing in our lives. Widowhood presents a Christian woman with an opportunity—a situation in which she can, with God's help, show the world that her God is of infinite worth, that he makes no mistakes, and that he upholds those who trust in him. The work of God can be displayed in us for his glory. In this way, our widowhood can be useful to the kingdom of God rather than being wasted.

THE UNDISTRACTED WIDOW

DON'T WASTE YOUR WIDOWHOOD

Two months after my husband died, I read an article by John Piper entitled "Don't Waste Your Cancer."[1] At the time, Piper had been recently diagnosed with prostate cancer. As I read and reread the article, it occurred to me that Piper's advice for not wasting cancer could be adapted to the situation of being widowed. This adaptation increased my joy in the Lord and gave me added hope that I could live out my days as a widow with purpose to the glory of God. I am thankful that God brought the article to my attention early in my widowhood, for it has helped me not to waste it. Based on what I learned from Piper, I came up with ten steps on how not to waste our widowhood.

1) *We will waste our widowhood if we do not believe it is designed for us by God.* God designed our widowhood, but this truth does not suggest that he is impervious to the suffering in our loss; all God's designs flow from his love for us. Our omniscient God knows the depths of our suffering, and he promises his comfort and care as we go through it. He purposes good things to come from it as we love him and trust him in it. God is enough. He is sufficient for every trial. He is to us all that we need as we seek him wholeheartedly.

2) *We will waste our widowhood if we believe it is a curse and not a gift.* Widowhood is a gift in the sense that it is an opportunity given by God in which we illuminate the world around us in the midst of a crooked and twisted generation, among whom we shine as lights in the world, holding fast to the word of life (see Philippians 2). Most people are terrified of death—theirs and their loved ones'. Exhibiting joy in the Lord in the midst of our sorrow is a powerful testimony to the grace and power of God. Our gift from God keeps on giving. When we seek him in our sorrow, we will find him, and he will give us himself. As we rest in him and his love, we will manifest the beauty of Christ.

3) *We will waste our widowhood if we seek comfort from anything other than God.* To be a recipient of God's particular care is a great and sweet privilege. Once we experience such intense and tender attention from God, we will crave more. He teaches us to keep our eyes on him so that in every trial we will instinctively look to him first and foremost. God alone is able to keep his promises, and he will never abandon us.

4) *We will waste our widowhood if we refuse to think about death.* Thinking about death makes us wise and realistic. If we are going on an extended trip, we make plans so that we can reach our destination. The planning process aids us in considering the realities of where we are going, what we will do when we get there, and who will be a part of that experience. When we die, we do not want to meet a God we do not know. Death for the Christian is a portal to heaven, and we want to think carefully about heaven before we get there. Doing so increases our joy as we immerse our thoughts in the anticipation of our great hope. In the meantime, contentment comes from accepting wherever God wants us today—whether staying here, serving him on this earth, or going home to heaven and serving him face-to-face.

5) *We will waste our widowhood if we think that "surviving" widowhood means a desperate search for another mate rather than cherishing Christ.* Whether God provides us with another husband is entirely his business. Nothing is too hard for him. He can easily bring someone to marry into our lives. But either way, we will waste our widowhood if we do not cherish Christ more than before.

6) *We will waste our widowhood if we spend too much time reading about widowhood and not enough time reading about God.* Many books on widowhood focus on us, on our pain, on our felt needs, and on what the world says we should do. Many of them offer false hope. We waste our widowhood if we do not pursue true hope by deepening our love for God and focusing on him in the midst of our grief.

7) *We will waste our widowhood if we let it drive us into solitude instead of deepening our relationships with unmistakable affection.* Widowhood provides us with an opportunity to reach out and love others through sacrificial service in imitation of Christ. Surely there is someone we can bless with our love and concern and through opportunities to help others in need. The love that God is pouring out into our grieving hearts can overflow into the lives of those around us. We can lavish others with our love the way God has lavished his love on us—through the sacrificial service of Christ. Let's look at the cross and remember God's great love for us, then go out and spread that love to lonely and hurting people.

8) *We will waste our widowhood if we grieve as those who have no*

hope. What does grief infused with hope in the Lord look like? Does it mean we never shed a tear? No, that would be stoical. Does it mean we don't miss a beat and carry on as if nothing has changed? No, that would be callous. We widows feel deeply the pain of loss and express it openly yet appropriately, but our grief is to be saturated with the knowledge and tender presence of our Lord. Because we are held in the arms of God, protected and provided for, we can rest in calm assurance of his great love and care. We are not alone, not abandoned. Our days can be filled with the Lord and his Word, and we can face the future with faith.

9) *We will waste our widowhood if we treat sin as casually as before.* Growth in holiness, and therefore increased happiness in the Lord, is part of the good that God can accomplish in our widowhood. The powerful presence of the Holy Spirit will give us the strength needed to put off sin and put on obedience. The greater our obedience to God, the more joy we will have in our hearts.

10) *We will waste our widowhood if we fail to use it as a means of witness to the truth and glory of Christ.* We can seize opportunities to tell others what God is doing in our lives. But even more than that, we can tell others what we have learned about who God is and how he works in suffering. Those around us need to hear of the mercy, grace, and kindness of God. All people desperately need to hear the gospel, and we can explain to them how the gospel works in bereavement, testifying as to how we found the Lord to be sufficient for our every need as we endured the loss of our husband.

The experience of widowhood need not go to waste! We can use it to magnify Christ.

HOPE THAT DOES NOT DISAPPOINT

Hope for the future starts now and continues a minute, an hour, from now, with tomorrow, and all the days after that. Where is your hope? What is your hope? Christ must be the object of your hope. We look to him—back at what he has done and forward to what he will do. And, for the present, the hope we have in Christ is an anchor for our souls. If you are in Christ, your hope is anchored in him. Nothing can ultimately shake you—not even widowhood. Keep your eyes on him in loving adoration and he will keep you to the end.

> For this reason, because I have heard of your faith in the Lord Jesus and your love toward all the saints, I do not cease to give thanks for you, remembering you in my prayers, that the God of our Lord Jesus Christ, the Father of glory, may give you a spirit of wisdom and of revelation in the knowledge of him, having the eyes of your hearts enlightened, that you may know what is the *hope* to which he has called you, what are the riches of his glorious inheritance in the saints, and what is the immeasurable greatness of his power toward us who believe, according to the working of his great might that he worked in Christ when he raised him from the dead and seated him at his right hand in the heavenly places, far above all rule and authority and power and dominion, and above every name that is named, not only in this age but also in the one to come. (Eph. 1:15–21)
>
> She who is truly a widow, left all alone, has set her *hope* on God and continues in supplications and prayers night and day. (1 Tim. 5:5)
>
> Now may our Lord Jesus Christ himself, and God our Father, who loved us and gave us eternal comfort and good *hope* through grace, comfort your hearts and establish them in every good work and word. (2 Thess. 2:16–17)

May these words of Frances Havergal be an inspiration to live for God without distraction in your widowhood:

> O fill me with your fullness, Lord,
> until my very heart o'erflow
> in kindling thought and glowing word,
> your love to tell, your praise to show.
>
> O use me, Lord, use even me,
> just as you will, and when, and where,
> until your blessed face I see,
> your rest, your joy, your glory share.[2]

Appendix 1

HOW TO HELP A WIDOW

Religion that is pure and undefiled before God, the Father, is this:
to visit orphans and widows in their affliction, and to keep
oneself unstained from the world.

JAMES 1:27

Reading a biblically sound book about widowhood—what widows struggle with and what their particular needs are—is a great way to begin learning how to relate to the widows in your life. Doing so will help you to understand the experience and challenges of widowhood. Your increased understanding will aid you in helping the widows in your life.

WHAT DOES IT MEAN TO VISIT?

Every widow is an individual. No one likes being lumped into a group and having assumptions made about them based on demographics. *The only way to truly help a widow is to get to know her.* This will take time and effort on your part. According to James 1:27, "visiting widows" is evidence that your commitment to the Lord Jesus Christ is real and results in compassionate ministry to those in need. It demonstrates that you are a doer, not just a hearer of the Word.[1]

The Greek word for *visit* can also be translated as "look after" or "care for." Visiting does not consist in dropping by to see a widow, saying hello, and then leaving. The fact that a widow may not be in dire financial need does not relieve you of your Christian duty to look after her. The Bible has much to say about ministering to one another besides the giving of money. We can discover how to help widows in other ways by searching the New Testament for the words "each other" and "one another."

When you visit, please do not go once with a potted plant and never come back. If you assume that she is fine just because she attends worship each Sunday, you are failing in your ministry to her. Regular visits at her home are the best way to fulfill the James 1 command. You will be able to observe if she has needs regarding her home and property. It is also the best way to know her and to interact with her so that she will feel comfortable divulging other needs. If she is living in an eldercare facility, do not assume all her needs are being addressed. It is good for her and good for the staff to know that multiple people are looking in on her. It is those residents with few or no visitors who are more likely to become the victims of elder abuse.

Widows usually have ample visitors during the first few weeks following their husband's death, but as time goes on, those initial visits drop off as people get caught up in their own lives. Mark your calendar and make a point of contacting her and planning some sort of visit. It is always a nice gesture to bring along a small, inexpensive gift. After you leave, your gift will remind her of your love and kindness. When her mind has difficulty focusing and remembering, the gift will help her remember you. After my husband died, a friend gave me a little basket full of fragrant soap. Each time I used it I thought of her and her kindness.

Many people are uncomfortable around bereaved persons particularly if they have not experienced the death of a close family member or friend. In the diagram Speaking Sensitively I've listed just a few examples of things to say and not to say to a widow.[2] If you are unsure of what to say, it is best to say only "I'm sorry." Gentle hugs often speak more eloquently than words.

SPEAKING SENSITIVELY

What *Not* to Say	What to Say
"Call me if I can do anything for you."	"I'd like to come over next week and bring dinner or mow your lawn. What day is good for you?"
"I know how you feel" (even if you yourself are a widow).	"This must be so hard for you. I'm so sorry."
"He's in a better place."	"He will be sorely missed."

"You're still young—you can marry again."	Nothing.
"We'll have you over for dinner sometime."	"Are you free for dinner next Thursday?"
"How are you?"	"I care about how you are doing, and I am praying for you."
"I'll stop by some day soon."	"May I drop by this week and stay for about a half hour?"
"You're strong; you'll be okay."	Nothing.
"God never gives you more than you can handle."	Nothing—unless she asks you about 1 Cor. 10:13 and you have a correct theological understanding of this text.
"This is a blessing in disguise."	Nothing.

Regarding the "What to Say" column, you will not say these things, of course, unless you truly mean them. Try to adjust your tone to how she seems when you are with her. Be even-tempered and avoid singing songs to a heavy heart or it will feel like your presence is a blast of wintry air (Prov. 25:20). An effervescent personality is a trial to a heavy heart. The Scriptures call us to weep with those who weep (Rom. 12:15)—if not tears at least a properly serious, calming demeanor.

You may be the only person a widow (who lives alone) speaks to that day or, perhaps, for several days. Try to gently encourage her and carefully remind her of God's love for her. A warm smile and kind words may cheer her heart for quite a while. In that first winter after my husband died, I remember going to the grocery store and being surprised at how cheering it was just to have someone smile at me.

If the widow you are caring for no longer drives a car and has few options for getting around, take her out. Studies show that people feel better physically and mentally when they are able to enjoy the outdoors. Ask her if she would like to go to an arboretum, a conservatory, or public gardens or even to a local greenhouse. If you live where winters are cold, it is cheering in the middle of winter to visit an indoor garden.

DO YOU KNOW WHERE YOUR MOTHER IS?

Adult children have an obligation from the Lord to care for widows in their family:[3]

The church should care for any widow who has no one else to care for her. But if she has children or grandchildren, their first responsibility is to show godliness at home and repay their parents by taking care of them. This is something that pleases God very much. But those who won't care for their own relatives, especially those living in the same household, have denied what we believe. Such people are worse than unbelievers. (1 Tim. 5:3–4, 8 NLT)

Many factors must be considered when a widow needs help from her children. The fact that children have a biblical responsibility to care for widowed parents does not mean that a widow should try to control what form that help will take.

Sometimes a widow moves out of her home to live with or near her children. If she makes a long-distance move, she may discover that her children are so busy with their lives that she feels lonelier than if she had remained in her home community. You might suggest that she remain near siblings and friends since they may more closely share her generational interests and concerns, and they may have more time to enjoy doing things with her. It may be necessary, however, for her to move near her children in order to ease their responsibility to care for her, especially if she is not in good health.

We widows must be careful of expectations we may have regarding what our children should or should not do for us. Before we ask for help, we best consider the ways in which our request will impact our children's lives, especially their marriages. Most adult children have homes and families of their own that need their effort and attention. I am not saying that we shouldn't ask them for help, but we need to do this carefully and wisely. I have watched as widows and widowers have been so full of their own desires that they trample on the feelings of their children. In some of these situations, serious harm has been done to the relationships.

ARE YOU HELPING TOO MUCH?

Having said all the above, I need to add that it is possible to help a widow too much if you tend to be someone who rescues people. I have found that it is always a good rule of thumb when helping any person not to routinely do more for them than they are able to do for themselves. We need to pray for and apply wisdom so that we are truly helping others and not fostering ungodly dependency. A Christian widow has Christ for her Savior. Your role is to come alongside her with appropriate love and support.

Appendix 2

THE LOCAL CHURCH AND ITS WIDOWS

Honor widows who are truly widows.

1 TIMOTHY 5:3

Both in the Old and New Testaments we find ample evidence of God's concern for widows and of a long-standing tradition among both Jews and Christians of provision for their care. Is this tradition alive and well today? Or is the church now exempt from its responsibility due to the provision of Social Security, government assistance, life insurance, and pensions? The existence of these forms of financial provision (tenuous as some now are) does not relieve the church of its duty to care for its widows especially those who are alone. Additionally, other needs besides financial concerns require care and attention.

From a biblical standpoint, the widows in a church are not only those whose husbands are dead.[1] A widow in Scripture is a woman bereft of male leadership in her home. She could be a single woman or a divorced woman. For women in any of these three categories, the church may be responsible for their welfare if their families cannot or will not care for them, especially in their later years. Some churches are exemplary in the care of their widows and older adults. In other churches, there is room for improvement.

RIGHT EMPHASES?

Where in Scripture do we find an emphasis on youth ministry comparable to the clear directives all through God's Word to care for widows, to set up an intentional, organized, and ongoing ministry to provide for their needs? We don't. But today such an emphasis prevails in many churches.

It seems to me the Scriptures put the responsibility for ministry to children and youth largely on their parents and extended families. It is only when there are no parents or family members available to care for them that the Scriptures command a specific ministry to orphaned children. I am not saying that youth ministry in the church is wrong, but I am saying that it is possible to overemphasize it both in terms of budgetary allotment and staffing priority. Perhaps some of the time and money spent on youth ministry could be diverted to the care of older adults in the congregation. (If there are no older adults that is a separate problem.)

The church today largely imitates our culture with an excessive focus on youth. Many congregations separate their parishioners into constituency groups, making someone's life stage his or her defining characteristic. However, a multiplicity of circumstantially identified subgroups within a congregation does not make a church. It seems better to design and implement intergenerational ministry within a congregation, mixing it up so that the younger and older people know and love and serve one another (see Ps. 71:18). According to the Scriptures, the congregation should function like a family, not a coalition of support groups.

GIVING AND GAINING

Ministry to widows isn't flashy fun like working with a youth group. Churches aren't likely to see too many widows sign up for tubing on the river or a rollicking day at an amusement park. Caring for widows requires sacrificial love and patience without much pleasure for the giver unless the giver values the chance to gain insights from a widow's life experience, courage in the face of death, and, it is hoped, maturity in the Lord. These character qualities are not valued by our culture nor by many churches whose target audience is under forty years of age.

It is true that not all older people have gained wisdom and integrity, but older men and women who have proved over the years to be faithful and growing in grace ought to be honored and imitated in their faith.

You shall stand up before the gray head and honor the face of an old man, and you shall fear your God: I am the LORD. (Lev. 19:32)

Gray hair is a crown of glory;
it is gained in a righteous life. (Prov. 16:31)

The glory of young men is their strength,
but the splendor of old men is their gray hair. (Prov. 20:29)

Commenting on Proverbs 20:29, Matthew Henry says:

Let not young people despise the old, for they are grave [serious/sober-minded], and fit for counsel, and, though they have not the strength that young men have, yet they have more wisdom and experience. God has put honour upon the old man; for his gray head is his beauty.[2]

In case our modern ears do not hear Henry's words rightly, his reference to "man" is inclusive of both genders.

HOME AND CHURCH

It is clear from Acts 6 (a picture of diaconal ministry) and 1 Timothy 5 that God cares for widows mainly through their families and the local church. The church steps in when the following circumstances exist: (1) the widow cannot provide for her own welfare; (2) she has no remaining family members, or her extended family is unable or unwilling to help; and (3) she qualifies spiritually for help from her church according to the guidelines in the Scriptures. If family members are professing Christians yet not helping their widows, they need to be educated if they are ignorant of their God-given responsibility. If they are unwilling to help, church discipline is in order because they are in clear violation of the Scriptures.

Commentators differ in their understanding of 1 Timothy 5:9–11 and its mention of a list of widows who must qualify to be enrolled. Some see the passage as simply a list of those widows who have no one else to care for them, so the church takes direct responsibility for their needs. Other commentators understand the list as an enrollment of widows who are fit for special ministry in the church.[3] There is general agreement that the church is not financially responsible for any and all widows in the congregation. Rather, the widow must be eligible both financially and spiritually. Kent Hughes remarks, "So the only widows who qualified for church support were those who *financially* qualified through destitution and *spiritually* qualified through godliness."[4] He adds, "Such real widows are found in every congregation, and they are our sacred obligation."[5] In his sermon series "Widows in the Church," John MacArthur states:

> Widows then by God's design are uniquely His concern. They receive from Him sincere pity and merciful treatment. And all those people who name the name of God and identify with Him should so treat widows in a manner that would be consistent with how God treats them. . . . The treatment of these women then was a watershed, was a test case for the love of Christ borne in the hearts of the Christian community. Their spiritual character, the demonstration of their devotion to Christ could be seen in how they cared for people who were desperately in need of that care. And I might add that this has been a part of the church's life throughout all of its history.[6]

May your heart and your church pass the test and be blessed as your devotion to Christ manifests itself in faithful ministry to the widows among you.[7]

Appendix 3

THE GOSPEL OF THE LORD JESUS CHRIST

Gospel is a word that means "good news." Here's the start of the good news: there is a God and he is real. The evidence is all around you. It jumps out at you from sky and tree and flower and the human body and mind and the entire created universe! Theologians call this evidence "general revelation." You have to work hard at denying God's existence when the whole universe is shouting evidence to the contrary (see Psalm 19).

God is a good God—perfect in his goodness. He is loving and kind toward all he has made.[1] An evidence of his kindness is shown in the special revelation he has given us called the Holy Scriptures or the Holy Bible. In the first book of the Bible, Genesis, God tells how he created the first man and woman. He put them in a perfect environment and withheld nothing from them except the fruit of a certain tree.

When confronted by the evil fallen angel, Satan, who masqueraded as a serpent, Adam and Eve succumbed to temptation and rebelled against God's clear command. Though Adam and Eve were created without sin, they chose to do what God told them not to do. Since then, *every* person born into the world has inherited from Adam this sinful nature (see Rom. 5:12). "None is righteous, no, not one; no one understands; no one seeks for God. All have turned aside; together they have become worthless; no one does good, not even one" (Rom. 3:10–12).

Our nature is to go our own way, suppress the truth, and disregard God's law. Because we do this, we are his enemies.

For the wrath of God is revealed from heaven against all ungodliness and unrighteousness of men, who by their unrighteousness suppress the truth.

For what can be known about God is plain to them, because God has shown it to them. For his invisible attributes, namely, his eternal power and divine nature, have been clearly perceived, ever since the creation of the world, in the things that have been made. So they are without excuse. For although they knew God, they did not honor him as God or give thanks to him, but they became futile in their thinking, and their foolish hearts were darkened. (Rom. 1:18–21)

Unless we are given a new nature through the work of God in our lives, we naturally rebel against him. This rebellion merits the penalty of everlasting death.

MORE GOOD NEWS

Because we are unable to keep God's law, God provided a Savior because he is rich in mercy and amazing in grace. "All we like sheep have gone astray; we have turned—every one—to his own way; and the LORD has laid on [Jesus Christ] the iniquity of us all" (Isa. 53:6). Jesus Christ, the sinless Son of God, lived a perfect life and died a perfect death to save God's people from an eternity in hell.

Those who are given grace to trust in Christ's substitutionary death for them on the cross are given the gift of eternal life. "Only those who are truly aware of their sin can truly cherish grace."[2] Grace is God's favor given to us even though we do not deserve it; even though our sin merits eternal punishment. Though the wages of sin is death (Rom. 6:23), we do not need to die spiritually if we acknowledge that we are sinners in need of the saving work of Jesus Christ. J. I. Packer puts it this way: "When Adam and Eve failed to obey the terms of the covenant of works (Gen. 3:6), God did not destroy them, but revealed his covenant of grace to them by promising a Savior (Gen. 3:15)."[3]

A covenant is a solemn promise. God promises that you can be his covenant child: "But to all who did receive [Jesus Christ], who believed in his name, he gave the right to become children of God, who were born,

184

not of blood nor of the will of the flesh nor of the will of man, but of God" (John 1:12–13).

Jesus Christ saves sinners through his death as the sacrificial Lamb of God. The sacrificial system of the Old Testament culminated in the final sacrifice for sin. Jesus was that final sacrifice—the Lamb of God. Only Jesus Christ, the God-man, met the requirements of God's law. His nature was sinless and he never sinned. He appeased the wrath of God against sinners by suffering the punishment that you and I should suffer because of our sin.

God sent his one and only Son into the world to die as a propitiation (atonement) for the sins of his people. This means "the sacrifice of Jesus on the cross satisfied the demands of God's holiness for the punishment of sin . . . so Jesus propitiated or satisfied God."[4] Because of Christ's great love for his people, he willingly died on the cross, was buried, and rose again on the third day. Those who belong to him will also be resurrected at the return of Christ to this world. Our bodies will be reunited with our spirits (which go to heaven when we die), and thus we will live with God forever. This is the good news!

LIFE AND DEATH

It is literally a matter of life and death for you to ask God to pour out his grace into your heart to enable you to believe the gospel. Forgiveness of sin and repentance—turning from your sin to God and seeking his will with all your heart—is crucial to experiencing the love of Christ. From the very beginning of his public ministry, Jesus preached saying, "Repent, for the kingdom of heaven is at hand" (Matt. 4:17). It is absolutely essential that you understand the gospel of Jesus Christ.

Your life depends on knowing, believing, and responding in faith to the gospel. The world will allure you with its seeming pleasures, your sinful nature will demand its own way, and the Devil will gladly lead you into deeper and deeper sin. If you persist in ignoring the gospel message, your apathy and enmity toward Christ will keep you on the wide road to destruction. But I pray that you, by the power of the Holy Spirit, will respond to the gospel. May you be eager to believe the Word of God and its message of salvation in Christ. Read, meditate, and pray through the letter of Paul to the Romans in the New Testament, particularly chapters 3 through 8, in order to gain a better understanding of the gospel of Christ.

Find a church that preaches and teaches the Bible so that you can talk to faithful Christians who can help you better understand the gospel and answer your questions and concerns. It may take some effort to find a church that does this consistently and faithfully. If the only faithful church you can find is far away, you can call and ask for a referral to a faithful church in your area. You need the ministry of the Word, the fellowship of other Christians, and the opportunity to live out your faith in the Lord through service to others. Hebrews 10:24–25 says, "Let us consider how to stir up one another to love and good works, not neglecting to meet together, as is the habit of some, but encouraging one another, and all the more as you see the Day drawing near."

A GOSPEL-GOVERNED LIFE

Of the gospel, Martyn Lloyd-Jones observes:

> There is no aspect of life but that the gospel has something to say about it. The whole of life must come under its influence because it is all-inclusive; the gospel is meant to control and govern everything in our lives.[5]

Does the gospel control and govern everything in your life? If not, do you aim to have all your life controlled and governed by it? None of us lives the Christian life perfectly; that is one of the reasons we so desperately need Christ. But our aim should be to live for Christ and to let the gospel control our lives.

Perhaps you consider yourself to be a good person. You go to church and you even pray sometimes. You read the Bible occasionally and do nice things for other people. But think about this:

> It is wrong to call [people] . . . Christian simply because they are doing good things and "following Jesus' example." To be a Christian, to be a partaker of the blessings of the Kingdom, requires one first to go through the gate—that is, to come to Christ in faith and be forgiven of sin and

atoned for. . . . A person can "live like Jesus lived" all he wants to, but unless he goes through the Wicket Gate[6] of atonement, faith and repentance, he's not really come to Christ.[7]

You see, our sin is a deeper problem than our suffering. Even the suffering that accompanies the death of a spouse is not as deep a problem as our sin against a holy God. I urge you, therefore, "Examine yourselves, to see whether you are in the faith. Test yourselves. Or do you not realize this about yourselves, that Jesus Christ is in you?—unless indeed you fail to meet the test!" (2 Cor. 13:5).

Jesus said, "All that the Father gives me will come to me, and whoever comes to me I will never cast out" (John 6:37). Go to him with a humble heart, confessing your sin, asking his forgiveness, and his promise is that he will never refuse you.

"I am the Alpha and the Omega, the first and the last, the beginning and the end." . . . He who testifies to these things says, "Surely I am coming soon." Amen. Come, Lord Jesus! (Rev. 22:13, 20)

SUGGESTED READING

Bakker, Frans. *Praying Always*. Carlisle, PA: Banner of Truth, 2004.

Baxter, Richard. *Dying Thoughts*. Edinburgh: Banner of Truth, 2004.

Boice, James Montgomery. *Living by the Book: The Joy of Loving and Trusting God's Word*. Grand Rapids, MI: Baker, 1997.

_____. *Psalms: An Expositional Commentary*. 3 vols. Grand Rapids, MI: Baker, 2005.

Bonar, Horatius. *When God's Children Suffer*. Grand Rapids, MI: Kregel, 1992.

Bridges, Charles. *A Modern Study in the Book of Proverbs: Charles Bridges' Classic Revised for Today's Reader*. Edited by George F. Santa. Milford, MI: Mott Media, 1978.

Bridges, Jerry. *The Crisis of Caring: Recovering the Meaning of True Fellowship*. Phillipsburg, NJ: P&R, 1985.

_____. *The Discipline of Grace: God's Role and Our Role in the Pursuit of Holiness*. Colorado Springs, CO: NavPress, 1994.

_____. *Trusting God: Even When Life Hurts*. Colorado Springs, CO: NavPress, 1988.

Broderick, Patti McCarthy. *He Said, "Press": Hearing God Through Grief*. Kearney, NE: Morris, 2004.

Brownback, Lydia. *Contentment: A Godly Woman's Adornment*. Wheaton, IL: Crossway, 2008.

_____. *Trust: A Godly Woman's Adornment*. Wheaton, IL: Crossway, 2008.

Burroughs, Jeremiah. *Learning to Be Happy*. London: Grace Publications Trust, 1988.

Carson, D. A. *A Call to Spiritual Reformation: Priorities from Paul and His Prayers*. Grand Rapids, MI: Baker, 1992.

_____. *How Long, O Lord? Reflections on Suffering and Evil*. Grand Rapids, MI: Baker, 1990.

Chalmers, Thomas. "The Expulsive Power of a New Affection." http://parish-pres.org/documents/The%20Expulsive%20Power%20of%20a%20New%20Affection.pdf (accessed May 1, 2009).

Clark, Jayne. *Loneliness*. Winston-Salem, NC: Punch Press, 2005.

Clarkson, Margaret. *Destined for Glory: The Meaning of Suffering*. Grand Rapids, MI: Eerdmans, 1983.

Duncan, J. Ligon. *Does Grace Grow Best in Winter?* Phillipsburg, NJ: P&R, 2009.

Edwards, Jonathan. *Altogether Lovely: Jonathan Edwards on the Glory and Excellency of Christ*. Edited by Don Kistler. Morgan, PA: Soli Deo Gloria, 1997.

Elliot, Elisabeth. *Discipline: The Glad Surrender*. Old Tappan, NJ: Revell, 1982.

_____. *Facing the Death of Someone You Love*. Wheaton, IL: Good News Publishers, 2006.

_____. *Loneliness: It Can Be a Wilderness*. Nashville, TN: Oliver Nelson, 1988.

_____. *A Path through Suffering: Discovering the Relationship between God's Mercy and Our Pain*. Ventura, CA: Regal, 1990.

Ferguson, Sinclair B. *Children of the Living God*. Carlisle, PA: Banner of Truth, 1989.

_____. *A Heart for God*. Colorado Springs, CO: NavPress, 1985.

Fitzpatrick, Elyse. *Because He Loves Me: How Christ Transforms Our Daily Life*. Wheaton, IL: Crossway, 2008.

_____. *Overcoming Fear, Worry, and Anxiety*. Eugene, OR: Harvest, 2001.

_____. *A Steadfast Heart: Experiencing God's Comfort in Life's Storms*. Phillipsburg, NJ: P&R, 2006.

Fitzpatrick, Elyse, and Carol Cornish. *Women Helping Women: A Biblical Guide to Major Issues Women Face*. Eugene, OR: Harvest, 1997.

Hadler, Nortin M. *Worried Sick: A Prescription for Health in an Overtreated America*. Chapel Hill, NC: University of North Carolina Press, 2008.

James, John Angell. *The Widow Directed to the Widow's God*. Morgan, PA: Soli Deo Gloria, 1996.

Jones, Robert D. *Forgiveness: I Just Can't Forgive Myself*. Phillipsburg, NJ: P&R, 2000.

Journal of Biblical Ethics in Medicine. http://www.bmei.org/jbem.

Lewis, C. S. *The Screwtape Letters*. Charlotte, NC: Commission Press, 1976.

Lloyd-Jones, D. Martyn. *The Christian Soldier: An Exposition of Ephesians 6:10 to 20*. Grand Rapids, MI: Baker, 1977.

_____. *The Christian Warfare: An Exposition of Ephesians 6:10 to 13*. Grand Rapids, MI: Baker, 1976.

_____. *Enjoying the Presence of God*. Ann Arbor, MI: Servant, 1992.

_____. *Let Not Your Heart Be Troubled*. Wheaton, IL: Crossway, 2009.

_____. *Spiritual Depression: Its Causes and Its Cure*. Grand Rapids, MI: Eerdmans, 1965.

_____. *The Unsearchable Riches of Christ: An Exposition of Ephesians 3:1 to 21*. Grand Rapids, MI: Baker, 1979.

Lundgaard, Kris. *The Enemy Within: Straight Talk about the Power and Defeat of Sin*. Phillipsburg, NJ: P&R, 1998.

MacArthur Jr., John. *Alone with God: The Power and Passion of Prayer*. Wheaton, IL: Victor, 1995.

_____. *The Glory of Heaven: The Truth about Heaven, Angels, and Eternal Life*. Wheaton, IL: Crossway, 1996.

_____. *Standing Strong: How to Resist the Enemy of Your Soul*. 2d ed. Colorado Springs, CO: Victor, 2006.

_____. *Twelve Extraordinary Women*. Nashville, TN: Thomas Nelson, 2005.

_____. *Why Believe the Bible: The Reliability of God's Word and Its Power to Transform Your Life*. Glendale, CA: Gospel Light, 1980.

_____. "Widows in the Church." Sermon series. http://www.gty.org/resources/Sermons/series/394.

Mahaney, C. J. *Living the Cross Centered Life: Keeping the Gospel the Main Thing*. Sisters, OR: Multnomah, 2006.

Murray, John J. *Behind a Frowning Providence*. Carlisle, PA: Banner of Truth, 1990.

Nichols, Stephen J. *Heaven on Earth: Capturing Jonathan Edwards's Vision of Living in Between*. Wheaton, IL: Crossway, 2006.

Peace, Martha. *Attitudes of a Transformed Heart*. Bemidji, MN: Focus, 2002.

Petty, James C. *Priorities: Mastering Time Management*. Phillipsburg, NJ: P&R, 2001.

Phillips, Richard D. *Walking with God: Learning Discipleship in the Psalms*. Carlisle, PA: Banner of Truth, 2005.

Pink, A. W. *Comfort for Christians*. Grand Rapids, MI: Ebenezer, 2003.

_____. *The Nature of God*. Chicago, IL: Moody, 1975.

_____. *The Sovereignty of God*. Carlisle, PA: Banner of Truth, 1928.

Piper, John. *Desiring God*. Portland, OR: Multnomah, 1986.

_____. "Fear Not, I Am with You, I Am Your God." Sermon. June 23, 1993. http://www.desiringgod.org/ResourceLibrary/Sermons/ByDate/1993/844 (accessed March 14, 2006).

_____. *Seeing and Savoring Jesus Christ*. Rev. ed. Wheaton, IL: Crossway, 2004.

_____. "There Is a Way to Be Happy Even in Sadness." March 23, 2005. http://desiringgod.org/ResourceLibrary/TasteandSee/ByDate/2005/1288 (April 1, 2005).

Powlison, David. *Facing Death with Hope: Living for What Lasts*. Greensboro, NC: New Growth, 2008.

_____. *Power Encounters: Reclaiming Spiritual Warfare*. Grand Rapids, MI: Baker, 1995.

_____. *Stress: Peace amid the Pressure*. Phillipsburg, NJ: P&R, 2004.

_____. *Worry: Pursuing a Better Path to Peace*. Phillipsburg, NJ: P&R, 2004.

Ryken, Philip Graham. *When You Pray: Making the Lord's Prayer Your Own*. Wheaton, IL: Crossway, 2000.

Shuman, Joel, and Brian Volck. *Reclaiming the Body: Christians and the Faithful Use of Modern Medicine*. Grand Rapids, MI: Brazos, 2006.

Sproul, R. C. *Knowing Scripture*. Downers Grove, IL: InterVarsity, 1977.

Spurgeon, Charles Haddon. *Joy in Christ's Presence*. New Kensington, PA: Whitaker, 1997.

_____. *Morning and Evening*. Peabody, MA: Hendrickson, 1995.

Tada, Joni Eareckson. *Heaven: Your Real Home*. Grand Rapids, MI: Zondervan, 1995.

Tada, Joni Eareckson, and Steve Estes. *When God Weeps: Why Our Sufferings Matter to the Almighty*. Grand Rapids, MI: Zondervan, 1997.

Tozer, A. W. *The Knowledge of the Holy*. New York, Harper & Row, 1961.

_____. *The Pursuit of God*. Camp Hill, PA: Christian Publications, 1982.

Tripp, Paul David. *Grief: Finding Hope Again*. Greensboro, NC: New Growth, 2004.

_____. *A Shelter in the Time of Storm: Meditations on God and Trouble*. Wheaton, IL: Crossway, 2009.

_____. *Suffering: Eternity Makes a Difference*. Phillipsburg, NJ: P&R, 2001.

_____. *Whiter Than Snow: Meditations on Sin and Mercy*. Wheaton, IL: Crossway, 2008.

VanDrunen, David. *Bioethics and the Christian Life: A Guide to Making Difficult Decisions*. Wheaton, IL: Crossway, 2009.

Vincent, Thomas. *True Christian's Love to the Unseen Christ.* Morgan, PA: Soli Deo Gloria, 2001.

Watson, Thomas. *The Art of Divine Contentment.* Edited by Don Kistler. Morgan, PA: Soli Deo Gloria, 2001

_____. *All Things for Good.* Carlisle, PA: Banner of Truth, 1986.

Welch, Edward. *Blame It on the Brain? Distinguishing Chemical Imbalances, Brain Disorders, and Disobedience.* Phillipsburg, NJ: P&R, 1998.

_____. *Running Scared: Fear, Worry, and the God of Rest.* Greensboro, NC: New Growth, 2007.

_____. *When People Are Big and God Is Small: Overcoming Peer Pressure, Codependency, and the Fear of Man.* Phillipsburg, NJ: P&R, 1997.

Whitney, Donald S. *Spiritual Disciplines for the Christian Life.* Colorado Springs, CO: NavPress, 1991.

NOTES

INTRODUCTION

1. John Angell James, *The Widow Directed to the Widow's God* (Morgan, PA: Soli Deo Gloria, 1996).

CHAPTER 1: BEGINNING, ENDING, AND BEGINNING AGAIN

1. If you are not sure what the gospel of Jesus Christ is, please see Appendix 3.

2. Frank Graeff, "Does Jesus Care?" 1901.

3. Dylan Thomas, *A Child's Christmas in Wales* (New York: Holiday House, 1985), 30.

4. A. W. Tozer, *The Pursuit of God* (Camp Hill, PA: Christian Publications, 1982), 92.

5. Geoff Thomas, "Singleness," sermon, Alfred Place Baptist Church, Aberystwyth, Wales, UK, http://alfredplace.simbahosting.co.uk/Sermons/Gen9.htm (accessed September 2, 2007), emphasis original.

6. Katharina von Schlegel, "Be Still, My Soul," 1752.

CHAPTER 2: IDENTIFYING YOURSELF ANEW

1. United States Census Bureau, *The 2008 Statistical Abstract*, "Women and Men Population in the United States: 2006." Table 2: "Marital Status of the Population 15 Years and Over by Age and Sex: 2006," http://www.census.gov/population/www/socdemo/men_women_2006.html (accessed September 12, 2008).

2. For a more complete discussion of identity in Christ see Elyse Fitzpatrick and Carol Cornish, eds., *Women Helping Women: A Bibilical Guide to the Issues Women Face* (Eugene, OR: Harvest, 1997), chap. 3.

3. D. Martyn Lloyd-Jones, *The Life of Joy and Peace: An Exposition of Philippians* (Grand Rapids, MI: Baker, 1999), 92.

4. Charles Wesley, "And Can It Be That I Should Gain?" 1739.

5. Isaac Watts, "When I Survey the Wondrous Cross," 1707.

6. Katharina von Schlegel, "Be Still, My Soul," 1752.

CHAPTER 3: TRUSTING GOD

1. Paul David Tripp, "Imagination," Part 1, http://www.paultrippministries.org/default2.aspx?pid=215 (accessed December 4, 2006).

2. Dr. and Mrs. Howard Taylor, *Hudson Taylor's Spiritual Secret* (Chicago: Moody, 1989), 177.

3. A. W. Pink, *The Nature of God* (Chicago: Moody, 1999), 61.

4. See Derek Kidner's comment on the meaning of "acknowledge" in Proverbs 3:6. He says, "Acknowledge is quite simply 'know,' which contains not only the idea of acknowledging, but the much richer content of being 'aware of,' and having 'fellowship with'" (*Proverbs: An Introduction and Commentary* [Downers Grove, IL: InterVarsity, 1964], 63–64).

5. Katharina von Schlegel, "Be Still, My Soul," 1752.

CHAPTER 4: CHERISHING CHRIST

1. George F. Santa, *A Modern Study in the Book of Proverbs: Charles Bridges' Classic Revised for Today's Reader* (Milford, MI: Mott Media, 1978), 318–19 (emphasis original).

2. If you are struggling with longings for the wrong things, I suggest you read two books by Elyse Fitzpatrick: *Idols of the Heart: Learning to Long for God Alone* (Phillipsburg, NJ: P&R, 2004) and *Because He Loves Me: How God Transforms Our Daily Life* (Wheaton, IL: Crossway, 2008).

3. J. C. Ryle, *Holiness* (Grand Rapids, MI: Baker, 1979), 127–28.

4. D. Martyn Lloyd-Jones, *The Unsearchable Riches of Christ: An Exposition of Ephesians 3:1 to 21* (Grand Rapids, MI: Baker, 1979), 41–42.

5. C. J. Mahaney, *Living the Cross Centered Life* (Sisters, OR: Multnomah, 2006), 15.

6. Katharina von Schlegel, "Be Still, My Soul," 1752.

CHAPTER 5: ENJOYING THE HOLY SPIRIT

1. Arthur Bennett, *The Valley of Vision* (Carlisle, PA: Banner of Truth, 1975), 28.

2. Mark Johnston, "I Believe in the Holy Spirit," http://www.reformation 21.org/articles/i-believe-in-the-holy-spirit.php (accessed January 7, 2009).

3. Charles H. Spurgeon, *Morning and Evening* (Peabody, MA: Hendrickson, 1995), 573.

4. James Montgomery Boice, *Psalms 42–106: An Expositional Commentary* (Grand Rapids, MI: Baker, 1996), 519.

5. Ibid., 128.

6. George Croly, "Spirit of God, Descend Upon My Heart," 1854.

CHAPTER 6: GAINING COMFORT FROM GOD'S WORD

1. You can access many hymnals on the Internet.

2. Mary A. Lathbury, "Break Thou the Bread of Life," 1877.

CHAPTER 7: LEARNING FROM BIBLICAL WIDOWS

1. John MacArthur Jr., *Twelve Extraordinary Women* (Nashville: Thomas Nelson, 2005), 137.

2. Ibid., 138–9.

3. You can read a similar story in 1 Kings 17:8–24 about the widow of Zarephath.

4. William Walsham How, "For All the Saints," 1864.

CHAPTER 8: LEARNING FROM CONTEMPORARY WIDOWS

1. Elisabeth Elliot, *Facing the Death of Someone You Love* (Wheaton, IL: Good News Publishers, 2006), 5–6.

2. Elisabeth Elliot, *The Elisabeth Elliot Newsletter* (Ann Arbor, MI: Servant, May/June 2000), 1 (emphasis original). Also available at http://www.elisabethelliot.org/newsletters/2000-05-06.pdf (accessed February 20, 2009).

3. Elisabeth Elliot, *Loneliness* (Nashville: Oliver Nelson, 1988), 36–37 (emphasis original).

4. Patti McCarthy Broderick, *He Said, "Press": Hearing God Through Grief* (Kearney, NE: Morris, 2004), 69.

5. Also see Elyse Fitzpatrick and Carol Cornish, eds., *Women Helping Women: A Biblical Guide to Issues Women Face* (Eugene, OR: Harvest, 1997), 546, for a checklist as a guide in choosing sound books. Check "The Discerning Reader" online for book reviews (http://www.discerningreader.com).

6. Folliott S. Pierpoint, "For the Beauty of the Earth," 1864.

CHAPTER 9: GRIEVING IN A GODLY WAY

1. Elyse Fitzpatrick and Carol Cornish, eds., *Women Helping Women: A Biblical Guide to the Issues Women Face* (Eugene, OR: Harvest, 1997), 491.

2. Leon Morris, *The First and Second Epistles to the Thessalonians* (Grand Rapids, MI: Eerdmans, 1991), 136.

3. Charles H. Spurgeon, *Morning and Evening* (Peabody, MA: Hendrickson, 1995), 141.

4. D. Martyn Lloyd-Jones, *The Unsearchable Riches of Christ: An Exposition of Ephesians 3:1 to 21* (Grand Rapids, MI: Baker, 1979), 66.

5. J. Wilbur Chapman, "Jesus! What a Friend for Sinners," 1910.

CHAPTER 10: MANAGING YOUR EMOTIONS

1. Jerry Bridges, *Trusting God* (Colorado Springs: NavPress, 1988), 140.

2. Patti McCarthy Broderick, *He Said, "Press": Hearing God Through Grief* (Kearney, NE: Morris, 2004), 39.

3. Ibid., 43.

4. While this situation would not be identical to utilizing a medium to communicate with the dead, Deut. 18:9–12 and Isa. 8:19 seem to indicate that any attempt to consult the dead is prohibited.

5. A discussion of whether those who are in heaven know what is happening to us here on earth is beyond the scope of this book. But the dead are no longer accessible to us as long as we are in this world.

6. Pastor Fred Zaspel, Reformed Baptist Church, Franconia, PA, e-mail message to the author, July 30, 2008.

7. D. Martyn Lloyd-Jones, *The Life of Joy and Peace: An Exposition of Philippians* (Grand Rapids, MI: Baker, 1999), 422–23.

8. If you have trouble identifying and labeling feelings, find lists of feelings and affective states online or in books about communication.

9. See D. Martyn Lloyd-Jones, *Spiritual Depression: Its Causes and Its Cure* (Grand Rapids, MI: Eerdmans, 1965), esp. chap. 8.

10. See Appendix 3.

11. John A. Younts, *Everyday Talk: Talking Freely and Naturally about God with Your Children* (Wapwallopen, PA: Shepherd Press, 2004), 140.

12. Kate B. Wilkinson, "May the Mind of Christ, My Savior," 1925.

CHAPTER 11: OVERCOMING LONELINESS

1. Derek Kidner, *Psalms 73–150: A Commentary*, Tyndale Old Testament Commentaries, ed. D. J. Wiseman (Downers Grove, IL: InterVarsity, 1973), 360.

2. Nancy Leigh DeMoss, "To Pursue or Not to Pursue," in *Seven Secrets for Singles* (http://www.reviveourhearts.com/radio/roh/today.php?pid=457), accessed June 3, 2003 (emphasis original).

3. Lydia Brownback, "Looking For Love on the Internet? Seven Things to Consider," The Purple Cellar blog, April 5, 2007, http://www.purplecellar.blogspot.com/search/label/dating.

4. B. Mansell Ramsey, "Teach Me Thy Way, O Lord," 1920.

CHAPTER 12: FACING YOUR FEARS

1. For a discussion of fear and anxiety, see Elyse Fitzpatrick, *Overcoming Fear, Worry, and Anxiety: Becoming a Woman of Faith and Confidence* (Eugene, OR: Harvest, 2001).

2. Sinclair Ferguson, "The Fear of the Lord," *Discipleship Journal* 52 (July–August 1989): 41.

3. See John Piper, sermon, "What Is the Recession For?" (http://www.desiringgod.org/ResourceLibrary/Sermons/ByDate/2009/3566/), accessed February 11, 2009.

4. Charles H. Spurgeon, *Morning and Evening* (Peabody, MA: Hendrickson, 1995), 488.

5. Some verses about fear: Pss. 3:6; 27:1; 34:4; 56:3–4, 11; 112:7–8; Prov. 3:24–25; Isa. 44:8; 51:12; Matt. 6:25–34; 8:26; 14:27, 30; John 14:1, 27; 2 Tim. 1:7.

6. William Cowper, "God Moves in a Mysterious Way," 1774.

CHAPTER 13: BATTLING YOUR ADVERSARY

1. Charles Spurgeon, *Morning and Evening* (Peabody, MA: Hendrickson, 1995), 128.

2. J. I. Packer, *Concise Theology: A Guide to Historic Christian Beliefs* (Carol Stream, IL: Tyndale, 1993), 67.

3. Spurgeon, *Morning and Evening*, 509.

4. William Cowper, "Exhortation to Prayer," in *The New Oxford Book of Christian Verse*, ed. Donald Davie (New York: Oxford University Press, 1981), 201.

5. A. W. Pink, *The Nature of God* (Chicago: Moody, 1999), 247, 249.

6. Sabine Baring-Gould, "Onward, Christian Soldiers," 1864.

CHAPTER 14: LEARNING TO BE CONTENT IN YOUR CIRCUMSTANCES

1. Philip Graham Ryken, *Exodus: Saved for God's Glory* (Wheaton, IL: Crossway, 2005), 673–74.

2. Read and meditate on these Scripture verses: Pss. 22:23–26; 119:10–16; Isa. 55:6–7; Jer. 29:11–14; Matt. 6:33; 7:7–8; Col. 3:1–3; Heb. 11:6.

3. See chap. 3 in Elyse Fitzpatrick and Carol Cornish, eds., *Women Helping Women: A Biblical Guide to the Issues Women Face* (Eugene, OR: Harvest, 1997).

4. Lydia Brownback, *Contentment: A Godly Woman's Adornment* (Wheaton, IL: Crossway, 2008), 24.

5. Charles Wesley, "Thou Hidden Source of Calm Repose," 1749.

CHAPTER 15: REMEMBERING THE PAST

1. You can view these paintings on the Internet at http://www.charleswysocki.com.

2. A widow's walk is a railed observation platform atop a house used for observing ships at sea.

3. James Montgomery Boice, *Psalms 42–106: An Expositional Commentary* (Grand Rapids, MI: Baker, 1996), 639.

4. Ibid., 641.

5. John Calvin, *Commentary on Philippians*, Christian Classics Ethereal Library (http://www.ccel.org/ccel/calvin/calcom42.iv.iv.iii.html), accessed June 5, 2009.

6. C. J. Mahaney, *Living the Cross Centered Life* (Sisters, OR: Multnomah, 2006), 26–27.

7. For a biblical view of self-forgiveness see the booklet by Robert D. Jones, *Forgiveness: I Just Can't Forgive Myself* (Phillipsburg, NJ: P&R, 2000).

8. Emily Brontë, "Remembrance"(http://www.poetry-online.org/bronte_emily_remembrance.htm), stanzas 4, 8 (accessed September 29, 2008).

9. Being your brother's keeper in this context means not doing something that will cause a weaker brother to stumble. See Rom. 14:1–15:7.

10. Isaac Watts, "Our God, Our Help in Ages Past," 1719.

CHAPTER 16: STRETCHING FORWARD

1. John Piper, "Discerning Idolatry in Desire" (http://wwwdesiringgod.org/ResourceLibrary/TasteAndSee/ByDate/2009/3991_Discerning_Idolatry_in_Desire/), accessed June 24, 2009 (emphasis original).

2. Thomas Chalmers, "The Expulsive Power of a New Affection," sermon (http://parishpres.org/documents/The%20Expulsive%20Power%20of%20a%20New%20Affection.pdf), accessed May 1, 2009.

3. Elisabeth Elliot, *Facing the Death of Someone You Love* (Wheaton, IL: Good News Publishers, 2006), 12.

4. Geoff Thomas, "The Marks of a Mature Christian," sermon, Alfred Place Baptist Church, Aberystwyth, Wales, UK (http://www.alfredplacechurch.org.uk/Sermons/phil27.htm), accessed February 15, 2006.

5. Joni Eareckson Tada, *Heaven: Your Real Home* (Grand Rapids, MI: Zondervan, 1995), 130–31.

6. Robert Murray McCheyne, "When This Passing World Is Done," 1837.

CHAPTER 17: DISTRACTION AND DEVOTION

1. Leon Morris, *The Gospel According to John*, rev. ed. (Grand Rapids, MI: Eerdmans, 1995), 489–90.

2. See Elyse Fitzpatrick, *Love to Eat, Hate to Eat* (Eugene, OR: Harvest, 2004).

3. See Heb. 10 and all the "one anothers" and "each others" in the New Testament.

4. Bernard of Clairvaux, "Jesus, Thou Joy of Loving Hearts," 1150.

CHAPTER 18: MAKING IMPORTANT DECISIONS

1. Peggy Parish, *Amelia Bedelia* (New York: HarperCollins, 1963).

2. A. W. Pink, *The Nature of God* (Chicago: Moody, 1999), 121–42.

3. Matthew Henry, *Commentary on the Whole Bible* (unabridged), CD-ROM, Accordance Bible Software, OakTree Software, 2004 (http://www.OakSoft.com) (emphasis original).

4. D. A. Carson, *The Love of God: A Daily Companion For Discovering the Riches of God's Word* (Wheaton, IL: Crossway, 1998), entry for September 2 (emphasis original).

5. Fanny Crosby, "All the Way My Savior Leads Me," 1875.

CHAPTER 19: NUMBERING YOUR DAYS WITH WISDOM

1. See Don Whitney's book *Spiritual Disciplines for the Christian Life* (Colorado Springs, CO: NavPress, 1991) for guidance on how to structure your days. Also see Richard Baxter's "How to Spend the Day with God" (http://www.puritansermons.com/baxter/baxter5.htm).

2. When Hezekiah was about to die, the Lord commanded him through the prophet Isaiah to set his house in order (see Isa. 38:1). God is a God of order, so we honor God when we conduct our affairs in an orderly manner (see 1 Cor. 14:40; Col. 2:5; and Titus 1:5).

3. E.g., see Daniel E. Deaton, "Questions Surrounding the Withdrawal of Artificial Hydration and Nutrition from Patients in a Persistent Vegetative State" (http://www.bmei.org/jbem/volume6/num3/deaton_questions_surrounding_the_withdrawal.php).

4. Fanny J. Crosby, "All the Way My Savior Leads Me," 1875.

CHAPTER 20: LEARNING FROM YOUR WIDOWHOOD

1. John Piper, "Don't Waste Your Cancer" (http://www.desiringgod.org/ResourceLibrary/TasteAndSee/ByDate/2006/1776_Dont_Waste_Your_Cancer/), accessed February 21, 2006.

2. Frances Havergal, "Lord, Speak to Me That I May Speak," 1872.

APPENDIX 1: HOW TO HELP A WIDOW

1. See Eidene Anderson, "Being a Learner," *Voice*, March–April, 2002 (http://www.ifca.org/home/140001498/140001500/Mar-Apr02.pdf?sec_id=140001500), accessed June 10, 2009.

2. You can find lists that are more extensive on various Web sites.

3. See Mollie Hemingway, "'Honor Thy Father' for Grownups: Or, How Not to Be a Deadbeat Son or Daughter," *Christianity Today*, July 1, 2009.

APPENDIX 2: THE LOCAL CHURCH AND ITS WIDOWS

1. John MacArthur Jr., sermon series: "Widows in the Church" (http://www.gty.org/resources/Sermons/series/394), accessed June 1, 2009.

2. Matthew Henry, *Commentary on the Whole Bible* (unabridged), CD-ROM, Accordance Bible Software, OakTree Software, 2004 (http://www.OakSoft.com).

3. For a good discussion of this issue see R. Kent Hughes, *1 and 2 Timothy and Titus* (Wheaton, IL: Crossway, 2000), 124–27.

4. Ibid., 125 (emphasis original).

5. Ibid., 126.

6. MacArthur, "Widows in the Church."

7. See article by Dana Williamson, "Church Finds Joy Serving Widows; Member Writes Instruction Book," *Baptist Press* (http://www.bpnews.net/bpnews.asp?ID=13920), accessed May 1, 2009.

APPENDIX 3: THE GOSPEL OF THE LORD JESUS CHRIST

1. E.g., see Psalm 145.

2. C. J. Mahaney, *Living the Cross Centered Life: Keeping the Gospel the Main Thing* (Sisters, OR: Multnomah, 2006), 88.

3. J. I. Packer, *Concise Theology: A Guide to Historic Christian Beliefs* (Carol Stream, IL: Tyndale, 1993), 87.

4. John MacArthur Jr., *The MacArthur Study Bible* (Nashville: Thomas Nelson, 2006), 1,935 (note on 1 John 2:2).

5. D. Martyn Lloyd-Jones, *Spiritual Depression: Its Causes and Its Cure* (Grand Rapids, MI: Eerdmans, 1965), 56.

6. A reference to John Bunyan's book *The Pilgrim's Progress*.

7. Greg Gilbert, "What Is the Gospel?—Tying It All Together" (http://blog.9marks.org/2008/09/what-is-the-g-3.html), accessed September 10, 2009.

GENERAL INDEX

Anna, 53–54

bitterness, 71
Boice, James, 53, 128
Bridges, Charles, 39
Bridges, Jerry, 87–88
Broderick, Patti, 72, 88–89
Brontë, Emily, 131–32
Brownback, Lydia, 100–101, 125

Calvin, John, 130
Carson, D. A., 60, 157
Chalmers, Thomas, 139
Comfort, in cyber relationships, 99–101; in evenings and weekends, 17–18; in other widows, 69–76, 173–75; in union with Christ, 119–20, 168–69
contentment, 120–25
Cowper, William, 115–16
creation, 48–49

dating, 99–102
death, 16, 169
decision making, 153–57
DeMoss, Nancy Leigh, 99–100, 102
depression, 91–93
Dunzweiler, Robert, 57

Elliot, Elisabeth, 21, 23, 70–73, 139

faith, 30–31
family relationships, 106, 164–65, 175–76
fears, 103–9
Ferguson, Sinclair, 104
financial security, 107–8
forgiveness, 131
friendships, 147–49
fruits of the Spirit, 120–21

funeral plans, 16–17, 162–63

God, and care for widows, 23–24, 67–68, 179–82, 186; devotion to, 25–26; glorifying, 87–91, 168, 170; images of, 49–50; promises of, 59–60, 81; sovereignty of, 83, 129; trust of, 29–35, 157
grace, 52, 80, 96, 104, 185
grandchildren, 133, 148
grieving, 78–85

happiness, 120–21
Havergal, Frances, 171
healthcare decisions, 161–62
heaven, 82–84, 139–41
Henry, Matthew, 156–57, 181
Holy Spirit, 30–31, 47–53, 91, 120–21, 152, 185
hope, 82, 170
hospice, 16
Hughes, Kent, 182
Husbands, communicating with after death, 89–90; honoring, 132–33; memories of, 133
hymns, 17–18, 58–59

idolatry, 33, 123, 138, 147
isolation, 105–6

James, John Angell, 13
Jesus, clinging to, 39–40; crucifixion of, 95–96; and distractions from following, 144–48; identity in, 22–23; resurrection of, 185
Johnston, Mark, 51
journaling, 77–78

keepsakes, 132–33

SCRIPTURE INDEX